# Managing Copyright
# in Higher Education

# Managing Copyright in Higher Education

## A Guidebook

Donna L. Ferullo

ROWMAN & LITTLEFIELD
*Lanham • Boulder • New York • London*

Published by Rowman & Littlefield
A wholly owned subsidary of The Rowman & Littlefield Publishing Group, Inc.
4501 Forbes Boulevard, Suite 200, Lanham, Maryland 20706
www.rowman.com

16 Carlisle Street, London W1D 3BT, United Kingdom

British Library Cataloguing in Publication Information Available

**Library of Congress Cataloging-in-Publication Data**

Ferullo, Donna L., 1957–
  Managing copyright in higher education : a guidebook / Donna L. Ferullo.
    pages cm
  Includes bibliographical references and index.
  ISBN 978-0-8108-9148-7 (cloth : alk. paper) — ISBN 978-0-8108-9149-4 (electronic)
1. Copyright—United States. 2. Library copyright policies—United States.
3. Academic libraries—Law and legislation—United States. 4. Universities and colleges—Law and legislation—United States. 5. Fair use (Copyright)—United States. 6. Intellectual property—United States. 7. Communication in learning and scholarship—United States. I. Title.
  Z642.F47 2014
  025.1'2—dc23

                                                                        2014019955

∞™ The paper used in this publication meets the minimum requirements of American National Standard for Information Sciences—Permanence of Paper for Printed Library Materials, ANSI/NISO Z39.48-1992.

Printed in the United States of America

For my parents, who truly represented the greatest generation. They considered their lives "ordinary," but in fact they were rather extraordinary. Typical of their generation, they did not dwell on their troubles but instead lived life to the fullest. Perseverance, laughter, and unconditional love are the keys to that full life. They are my inspiration, and I miss them every minute of every day.

# Contents

# Table and Figures

# Preface

Copyright impacts many areas of higher education both from an owner and a user perspective. On many campuses there is no copyright expert to turn to for advice and assistance in not only navigating the copyright law and understanding how the courts have interpreted the various provisions of the copyright law but also in applying it to real-life situations.

*Managing Copyright in Higher Education: A Guidebook* provides a basic understanding of the copyright law and strategies to consider when faced with copyright issues on campus.

The intended audience includes librarians, attorneys, faculty, students, administrators, and other staff primarily in higher education but also in the K–12 realm who grapple with copyright issues on a daily basis. It is also an excellent resource for library school programs in their foundational and management courses.

The book is developed from the perspective of a director of a copyright office and discusses approaches to resolving the broad range of questions that are encountered by such an office. It also provides information on how to establish a campus copyright office and the role of a copyright officer within the institution.

The book covers a wide range of topics related to the different constituencies in higher education. It specifically addresses issues for each category of user. Librarians will find discussions on digital issues, preservation, interlibrary loan, e-reserves, e-books, licenses, institutional repositories, and deeds of gift. In the faculty section, copyright is front and center in both teaching and research. How copyrighted works can be used in a classroom as well as online and through a course management system will be addressed. Faculty are not only users of copyrighted works but are owners as well. Publishing contracts; open-access initiatives and mandates; and the control, access, and ownership of data drive many copyright decisions for faculty. Students, particularly graduate students who are required to produce a thesis or dissertation, have some similar copyright issues to faculty but also some unique ones as well. They encounter copyright issues in course projects that then blend into potential career possibilities. Social media has become an integral part of life for many students, but few realize the copyright pitfalls associated with it. This section includes discussions on real-life copyright scenarios for students who use social media that blend educational and personal use of copyrighted works. Administrators and staff in disability resources offices, marketing and media services, printing services, and publishing are only a few areas that have to resolve copyright issues. This section will detail the most common copyright questions encountered by such departments and suggest options for resolution.

*Managing Copyright in Higher Education: A Guidebook* looks at the application of the copyright exceptions for education and libraries as well as the fair-use exception. It puts the exceptions in context for real-life situations. It provides the reader with questions to consider when confronted with a specific copyright issue and gives them a new perspective on the topic, all the while looking at how the current law and recent court cases might impact their thought processes. Copyright is increasingly becoming part of our daily lives in higher education, and it is important to understand how to approach the issues to achieve the results that are needed. This book will help readers reach that goal.

# 1

# Introduction to Intellectual Property

Copyright controls the ownership and use of creative works such as books, images, videos, music, and computer programs. Copyright not only protects printed works but digital ones as well. Questions abound as to whether copyright law is applied in the same manner to a digital work that was once only in print. Are the rules the same? Copyright is about balancing the rights of the copyright holder with the rights of the public to use the work. There can be a struggle to strike the proper balance. The U.S. Copyright Act[1] lags behind the rapidly changing technology, which makes it difficult to determine how the laws apply in a given situation. There are sections of the copyright law that appear to conflict with one another, so how does one resolve such a conflict? What happens when the U.S. Copyright Act conflicts with other federal laws or international treaties and agreements? Social media has changed the way we communicate and share information. How does copyright work with Facebook, YouTube, and Twitter? All of these issues will be tackled in later chapters.

Copyright plays a pivotal role in higher education and the advancement and sharing of knowledge. Education no longer consists solely of a professor and students meeting three times a week for fifty-minute sessions in a classroom on campus. Technology has been a game changer in higher education. Many courses are a hybrid model with a traditional classroom setting and an added online component controlled through course management systems. Some courses are taught only online in an asynchronous environment. MOOCs (massive open online courses) are trending right now, and the use of copyrighted works in those courses raises many interesting copyright questions. In the world today educators collaborate across disciplines and countries, making the interpretation and application of copyright laws a challenge.

International copyright law is front and center of many copyright discussions on campus, especially since it appears that there are no borders in the digital world. Which country's law applies when you have a professor in the United States and students in China and Dubai? Or when professor and students are all in countries outside the United States but the educational institution is based inside the United States? Faculty confront copyright issues not only in their teaching but in their research as well. They use other people's intellectual output and incorporate that into their own publications ranging from the traditional print books and journal articles to blogs, PowerPoint presentations, and other electronic resources. How do they apply copyright law in those different situations?

Students face copyright challenges as well, and many times they are not even aware of it. They create new works in the course of their studies, which may be protected under certain exceptions in the copyright law, then they graduate and the rules change. They no longer have the same copyright options available to them. How does a university teach students about their rights and responsibilities outside of the prescribed curriculum?

Staff and administrators are also responsible for understanding and applying copyright in a myriad of situations. It can range from information technology professionals responsible for responding to copyright infringement claims on the university network to secretaries being directed to copy entire books either to a paper format or scanning them into an electronic document. There are numerous copyright issues that crop up across the broad spectrum of daily activities that take place within a university.

The constantly changing role of libraries and the increasing use of licenses controlling the terms of use of copyrighted materials offer additional challenges. Libraries are constantly reinventing themselves to stay relevant in today's world. There are libraries that are removing printed books from their shelves and not purchasing other print material. Instead they are relying on electronic resources. How does copyright apply when the library does not own the physical copy of the book but only licenses an electronic copy? Libraries are actively engaged in small and sometimes mass digitization projects. How does copyright work in those situations? Library copyright issues are proliferating at lightning speed. Once upon a time libraries and universities were considered safe from copyright lawsuits, but now that is no longer the case. Copyright litigation is more complex than ever and casting an ever-widening net.

Questions abound, but finding answers can sometimes be difficult unless there is a copyright expert on staff. A question on the use of a copyrighted work can appear quite simple at first, but then, upon further analysis, is not. Trying to resolve a copyright issue is similar to peeling an onion one layer at a time.

An understanding of the basics of copyright is necessary before one can apply the law to a specific scenario. The law is complex and can appear contradictory at times. However, a fundamental grounding in the basics of copyright law and the rationale behind it is a prerequisite to any interpretation and application of it. Many in-depth treatises have been written about all sections of the copyright law. This book does not endeavor to emulate those works. Instead, it is an attempt to selectively analyze and apply critical sections of the Copyright Act that a copyright practitioner in higher education encounters on a daily basis. It is a bridge between the theoretical and the practical.

## INTELLECTUAL PROPERTY

The law recognizes several types of property, such as real property, which could be a house or land. There's personal property, such as an automobile, jewelry, your great-grandmother's set of china. It is something tangible that can be identified. Intellectual property is someone's creative output. It is an intellectual activity that results in a product.

Intellectual property has three major categories: copyright, patent, and trademark, including trade secrets. In some instances the right of publicity is also considered part of intellectual property law. Many times these areas over-

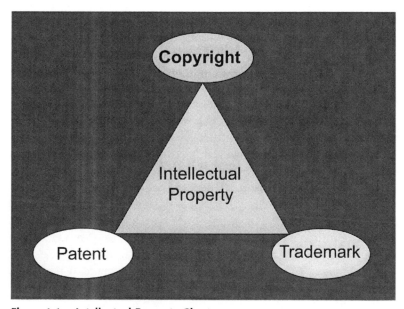

**Figure 1.1. Intellectual Property Chart**

lap, so it's good for the copyright practitioner to have a basic understanding of each of them. Copyright will be discussed in more depth throughout the book.

There are three different types of patents that one can apply for: utility, design, and plant. Utility patents are generally the most common type of patents and cover the way something is made and used, such as an automobile. It needs to be new and useful. A design patent protects the way something looks, like a piece of furniture. It's fairly obvious that plant patents protect plants but only ones that are new and distinct and that are asexually reproduced, like hybrid flowers or trees. Patents are not a new concept. In 1849 Abraham Lincoln invented a "method of steering a boat through shallow waters."[2] To date, he is the only U.S. president to hold a patent.

The United States Patent and Trademark Office (USPTO) is the federal agency that reviews and grants patent applications. Inventors are granted limited time for exclusive rights to their patents. Utility and plant patents receive twenty years of protection and design patents get fourteen years. Once the term has expired anyone can make the item or sell the product. For example, pharmaceutical companies have patents on their drugs, but when the patent expires any drug company can make their own version of it, subject to rules and regulations, of course, but the expiration allows for generic brands to become part of the market.

Patent law is a federal law and recently underwent a major overhaul. The Leahy-Smith America Invents Act[3] was enacted on September 16, 2011. Provisions of the new Act were staggered as to when they went into effect. Some of the major changes did not begin to occur until March 2013. The new patent law has many significant changes, but one in particular has really shifted the way companies, including universities, do business. In the United States, inventors could receive patents if they were the first to invent something and it was recognized by the USPTO as such. However, the new law recognizes the first to file, not the first to invent. The first-to-file system is utilized in most other countries, so the United States is now in sync with the rest of the world.

Trademarks and service marks protect a name, symbol, or device that identifies the source, quality, and ownership of a product or service. The mark distinguishes the product from others. Under trademark law, slogans are also protected, like Nike's "Just do it." Marks are not protected if they are generic or only a description of products or services. Kleenex is a brand, but *tissues* is the generic name. Marks are incredibly important and valuable to businesses. Consumers associate the reliability and trustworthiness of products by their marks, which is why companies will vigorously defend any copycats that can weaken their mark. This is referred to as diluting the mark. A trademark infringement claim can ensue when there are similar marks in the marketplace that create a likelihood of confusion.

The Lanham Act[4] is the federal law that protects trademarks for marks that are used in interstate commerce. Marks can also be registered in the states in which they are used. Generally, marks are protected from the date of first public use. Trademarks do not have to be registered, but there are additional benefits if they are, such as pursuing infringement claims in federal court. Marks can be registered for an initial ten years and then for additional ten-year periods as long as the mark is in use. Trademarks, like patents, are registered with the USPTO.

Trade dress can sometimes be considered part of a trademark. The way a package is designed or the colors or lettering associated with it that helps consumers identify a product is considered trade dress. It goes to the uniqueness of the design.

A trade secret is a valuable piece of information that if discovered by the competitors could severely impact a business. An example of this would be the recipe for Coca-Cola. There are no federal laws that protect trade secrets, but there are actions that can be taken under state laws. Many times they are contract-based disputes, such as a violation of a nondisclosure or noncompete agreement. Employers have employees sign these agreements to protect the assets of the business, such as the Coca-Cola recipe. It has been estimated that Coca-Cola's trademarks and related intellectual property are valued in excess of $70 billion dollars.[5]

The right of publicity can be considered a form of intellectual property law. Such a right protects someone's persona or image. Right-of-publicity laws are state based and can include protection of someone's voice, handwriting, image, mannerisms, and so forth. The term of protection varies from state to state. As of this writing Indiana[6] has the longest term of any state, which is protection during the individual's lifetime and one hundred years after the individual's death for those that died after the Indiana statute was enacted in 1994.[7] The right of publicity is generally associated with celebrities who license the use of their persona for commercial activities.

## THE LEGAL ARENA

There are three branches of the U.S. government: the legislative, the judicial, and the executive, as shown in figure 1.2. On the federal level, the legislative branch is Congress, which passes the laws. The judicial branch interprets the laws, and then the executive branch implements and enforces the laws enacted by Congress.

Under the executive branch, the federal agencies that are responsible for intellectual property are the U.S. Patent and Trademark Office (USPTO)

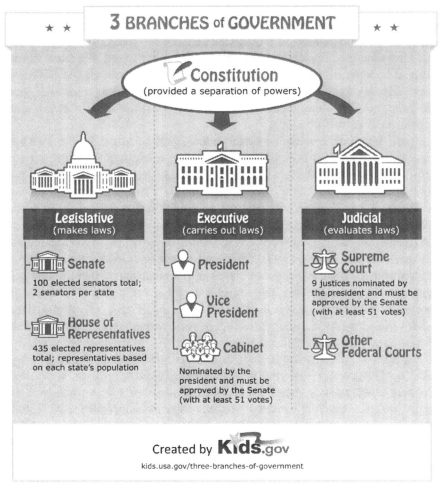

**3 BRANCHES of GOVERNMENT**

**Constitution**
(provided a separation of powers)

**Legislative**
(makes laws)

**Executive**
(carries out laws)

**Judicial**
(evaluates laws)

**Senate**
100 elected senators total;
2 senators per state

**House of Representatives**
435 elected representatives
total; representatives based
on each state's population

**President**

**Vice President**

**Cabinet**
Nominated by the
president and must be
approved by the Senate
(with at least 51 votes)

**Supreme Court**
9 justices nominated by
the president and must be
approved by the Senate
(with at least 51 votes)

**Other Federal Courts**

Created by **Kids**.gov
kids.usa.gov/three-branches-of-government

Figure 1.2.    Branches of Federal Government

for patents and trademarks and the U.S. Copyright Office for copyright. The Copyright Office is a department within the Library of Congress and is charged with administering and sustaining the national copyright system.

There are two areas of law—statutory law and case law. Statutory law is the law that is passed by legislatures. In the federal realm, the U.S Congress is responsible for statutory law. Federal laws are applicable to all states. State laws are passed by the state legislatures and are only valid in their respective states. As shown in figure 1.3, some intellectual property is protected by federal laws and others by state laws. At times it can seem that there are dueling

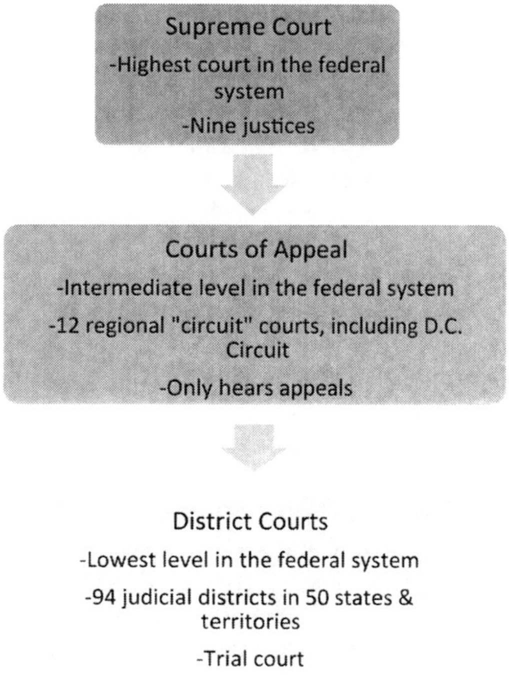

**Supreme Court**

-Highest court in the federal system

-Nine justices

**Courts of Appeal**

-Intermediate level in the federal system

-12 regional "circuit" courts, including D.C. Circuit

-Only hears appeals

**District Courts**

-Lowest level in the federal system

-94 judicial districts in 50 states & territories

-Trial court

**Figure 1.3.   Federal Court System**

laws. So which takes precedent? Generally, federal law takes priority over state law if the controversy is the same.

If there is a dispute that arises out of the statutory law, then such disputes are litigated in court. The judicial opinions result in case law. As with laws there is a division between federal and state court systems. If it's a federal law that's in question, then generally the controversy is litigated in federal courts, and state laws are litigated in state courts. Federal courts have three levels. The first level is the district court and that is the trial court. There are eighty-nine district courts distributed across the fifty states. If the losing party in the trial court wants to challenge the court's decision, then they file an appeal to the Federal Appeals Courts. The appeals courts are divided up into circuits whereby states are grouped geographically. There are thirteen judicial circuits. Decisions rendered in each circuit are only valid for the states that are part of that circuit. For example, the First Circuit is comprised of Maine, New Hampshire, Massachusetts, and Rhode Island. A ruling in the Second Circuit, which includes New York, would not be valid in the states served by the First Circuit. However, if another circuit has never heard a case with similar issues, which is called a case of first impression, then they can look at the legal reasoning of a circuit that has ruled on such a case, although they are not bound to follow that decision. Losses in the appellate courts can only be appealed to the U.S. Supreme Court, which is the highest court in the land. Only cases that raise a dispute about a constitutional issue are eligible to be argued before the Supreme Court. Once the Supreme Court hands down a decision, then all courts must follow the ruling. However, the Supreme Court picks and chooses which cases they will hear. They are not obligated to accept every case brought before them.

Another twist in legal disputes is the Eleventh Amendment to the U.S. Constitution, which provides sovereign immunity to states and state agencies. This means that states cannot be sued in federal court for money damages. Copyright is a federal law, so any controversy must be litigated in federal court. Public universities are state entities, so theoretically they cannot be sued in federal court for copyright infringement claims. However, they can be sued for other legal remedies such as injunctions, which would require that they stop the action in question. Criminal actions can also be brought against them if they willfully disregarded the law.

International law also plays a role in intellectual property law, specifically copyright law. In 1989 the United States became a signatory to the Berne Convention for the Protection of Literary and Artistic Works,[8] which is an international treaty on copyright. In order to be a part of Berne, the United States had to make changes to the U.S. Copyright Act, which will be discussed in a later chapter. The goal of Berne is to protect international copyright by requiring that member nations provide the same treatment under their copyright laws to nationals of other member nations. This is referred to as national treatment. Another player on the international stage is the World Intellectual Property Organization (WIPO), an agency of the United Nations. WIPO has always tended to favor content holders rather than users, but in 2013 the member nations did agree to move forward in providing access of print materials to the blind and visually challenged. The United States is also a party to trade agreements such as the North American Free Trade Agreement (NAFTA),[9] which includes the United States, Canada, and Mexico. NAFTA directly impacts how foreign works are protected in the United States. In 1994, Congress passed and President Clinton signed the Uruguay Round Agreements Act (URAA)[10] as part of the Uruguay Round Trade Agreements, which led to the creation of the World Trade Organization (WTO) in 1995. The WTO requires its members to provide a certain minimum level of protection for copyrights, patents, and trademarks. Whether they are international treaties, trade agreements, or membership in world organizations, the goal is the harmonization of copyright laws around the world.

Intellectual property is big business. In 2012, the U.S. Department of Commerce issued a report on intellectual property and the U.S. economy. They found that "IP-intensive industries accounted for about $5.06 trillion in value added, or 34.8 percent of U.S. gross domestic product (GDP), in 2010."[11] It is not only domestic but international trade in intellectual property products that generates large amounts of money. "Nearly $126 billion of U.S. exports now depend on some form of intellectual property protection."[12] The stakes are high when encountering intellectual property issues. It becomes even more important to understand the law and its practical application.

## NOTES

1. U.S. Copyright Act, 17 U.S.C. § 101 et seq.
2. Deborah E. Bouchoux, *Intellectual Property: The Law of Trademarks, Copyrights, Patents, and Trade Secrets* 4th ed. (Clifton Park, NY: Delmar Cengage Learning, 2013), 11.
3. Leahy-Smith America Invents Act, Pub.L. 112–29, 125 Stat. 284 (2011).
4. The Lanham Act, Pub.L. 79–489, 60 Stat. 427 (1946), 15 U.S.C. § 1051 et seq.
5. Bouchoux, *Intellectual Property*, 11.
6. Rights of Publicity, Ind. Code § 32-36-1-8(a).
7. Dillinger, LLC v. Electronic Arts, Inc., 795 F. Supp. 2d 829 (USDC S.D. Indiana, 2011).
8. Berne Convention for the Protection of Literary & Artistic Works Implementation Act, Pub. L. 100–568, Stat. 102 (1988).
9. North American Free Trade Agreement Act, Pub. L. 103–182, Stat. 107 (1993).
10. Uruguay Round Agreements Act, Pub.L. 103–465, Stat. 108 (1994).
11. Economics and Statistics Administration and the United States Patent and Trademark Office, *Intellectual Property and the U.S. Economy: Industries in Focus* (Washington, DC: U.S. Department of Commerce, 2012), vii. Accessed April 10, 2014. http://www.uspto.gov/news/publications/IP_Report_March_2012.pdf.
12. Bouchoux, *Intellectual Property*, 11.

# 2

## Copyright Basics

### U.S. COPYRIGHT LAW BASICS

In the very early days, the printing industry was controlled by churches and governments. There was no easy way to make a copy of a work except by painstakingly copying it by hand. However, with the invention of the printing press around 1450, the publishing business took off. No longer would books have to be produced by hand but now there was a machine that could crank out what were considered at that time perfect copies of books. Such innovation caused great concern to the entities that controlled what works could be published. Printers in England became concerned that they would lose control over the production and dissemination of their books so they sought protection from Parliament. Authors or creators of the works had virtually no rights, and they also raised their voices to Parliament for more protection from printers as well as a share in the financial interests of their works. Parliament enacted the first copyright law, called the Statute of Anne[1] in 1710. The statute provided authors with the right to control the copying of their works. The printers/publishers were only allowed to retain the copyright for fourteen years instead of perpetual rights, which is what they had prior to the statute. Most early American law is based on English law, so the Statute of Anne is the foundation of U.S Copyright law.

Copyright in the United States had its beginning with the U.S. Constitution. Article 1, section 8, clause 8 of the Constitution states that

Congress shall have the power . . . to promote the Progress of Science and Useful Arts, by securing for limited Times to Authors and Inventors exclusive Right to their respective Writings and Discoveries.[2]

This section of the Constitution also refers to patents, which we discussed in the previous chapter. The purpose of copyright is to encourage the citizens to be creative and to share the works. The signers of the Constitution believed that a successful democracy was comprised of an informed citizenship.

The first copyright law was enacted in Congress in 1790. There have been four major overhauls to the copyright law in 1831, 1870, 1909, and 1976. The U.S. Copyright Act of 1976 is the prevailing law today. There have been amendments to the 1976 law since it was implemented in 1978, but they are only changes to different sections within the act. Maria Pallante, the current (2014) register of the U.S. Copyright Office, has stated that she believes that it is time for the present Act to undergo a major overhaul calling it the next great copyright act.[3] She has undertaken a campaign to engage Congress in the discussions and to review what changes might need to occur.

The Copyright Act is all about balancing the rights of creators of works with the rights of the public to use that work. Often it is a struggle as how to determine what takes precedence. There are exceptions within the law that take into account the special circumstances that require various groups such as libraries and educators to have more leeway in their use of copyrighted works. The exceptions will be discussed in detail below.

Works are automatically protected under the Copyright Act from the moment of their creation if they are "original works of authorship" and are "fixed in any tangible medium of expression."[4] But what does that actually mean? An original work means that it is not an exact replica of someone else's work and that there is some creativity to it. There have been court cases over the years that have defined what is original and creative and sometimes even more importantly, what is not. One of the first cases handed down by the Supreme Court in 1884 involved Oscar Wilde, the Irish author and poet.[5] Wilde posed for famous photographer Napoleon Sarony, and a lithograph company, Burrow-Giles, sold unauthorized lithographs of the photo. The company claimed that there was no originality in the photo, thus no copyright attached to it, but the Court disagreed. Sarony had taken great care in choosing the costume Wilde posed in as well as the lighting, the facial expression, and the pose itself. Over one hundred years later in 1999, the Southern District Court of New York ruled in *Bridgeman Art Library, Ltd. v. Corel Corporation* that a photographic reproduction of an artwork did not have the requisite originality to engender copyright protection.[6] Another example is the Supreme Court case of *Feist Publications Inc. v. Rural Telephone Service Co.*,[7] whereby the Court ruled that an alphabetical listing of names in a white pages telephone directory did not pass muster on creativity. However, in the 1993 Eleventh Circuit case of *BellSouth Advertising & Publishing Corporation v. Donnelly Information Publishing, Inc.*,[8] originality and creativity were found in grouping businesses into categories in a yellow pages directory. The bar is quite low on what courts will find to be creative and original.

The second prong to establishing copyrightability in a work is the requirement of fixation in a tangible medium of expression. The work must be fixed in a physical form that can be "perceived, reproduced or otherwise communicated, either directly or with a machine or device.[9] It must also be available longer than a transitory duration. For example a video, sound recording, or book (either print or electronic) would be considered fixed. However, an extemporaneous speech that was not recorded would not be copyrightable, thus not eligible for protection under the Copyright Act. Once fixation and originality are attached to the work, then it is copyrightable.

There are eight categories of works that have been identified under the law as being eligible for protection.[10] They are:

1. Literary works
2. Musical works, including any accompanying words
3. Dramatic works, including any accompanying music
4. Pantomimes and choreographic works
5. Pictorial, graphic, and sculptural works
6. Motion pictures and other audiovisual works
7. Sound recordings
8. Architectural works

Literary works can include traditional works such as fiction and nonfiction, poetry, and dissertations as well as computer programs, games, and pamphlets. Pictorial, graphic, and sculptural works also include maps and charts. Sound recordings can be a series of musical, spoken, or other sounds. The categories are fairly broad but encompass quite a large number and many types of works.

Equally as important as what is covered is what does not have protection under the Copyright Act.[11] Ideas are not protected. It is the expression of the idea that generates the protection. For example, a common plot for novels and stories is a tragedy involving star-crossed lovers. The idea is certainly not new or unique, but the expression of it such as in *Romeo and Juliet* or *West Side Story* is, and that is protectable. Facts such as standard calendars or the periodic table of elements are not copyrightable. Titles, short phrases, typographical designs, and listings of ingredients such as for recipes are not protected. Slogans are also not protected under copyright, but they can be protected under trademark law. U.S. federal government works that are produced by employees within the scope of their employment do not have any copyrights attached to them. For example, photographs of state parks produced by the Department of the Interior, a report from the Department of Education on best methods for promoting science and math in elementary schools, or the food pyramid/plate from the Department of Agriculture are not copyrightable. Congress did not extend protection to sound recordings until February 15, 1972, so sound recordings made prior to that date are protected by state laws but not by the federal copyright law. Works that have expired copyrights are no longer protected. The duration of copyright and how a copyright expires will be discussed below. Works that are not protected by copyright are in the public domain, which means that they can be freely used without paying royalties or asking permission.

Once a work meets all the requirements for copyrightability, it is automatically protected under the 1976 Copyright Act. Prior to that act, a work had to be registered with the U.S. Copyright Office. If the work was not registered, then it would become a public domain work. Another major difference with the 1976 act is that works are protected from the moment of creation, not publication. Unpublished works did not receive federal protection until the 1976 statute. Up until that point, they were protected by state common law and the copyright never expired.

Owners of copyrighted works have exclusive rights subject to the exceptions noted above. An exclusive right gives the copyright holder the authority to control the use of their work. The Copyright Act provides owners with the following rights:[12]

1. to reproduce the copyrighted works in copies or phonorecords;
2. to prepare derivative works based upon the copyrighted work;
3. to distribute copies or phonorecords of the copyrighted work to the public by sale or other transfer of ownership, or by rental, lease, or lending;
4. in the case of literary, musical, dramatic, and choreographic works, pantomimes, and motion pictures and other audiovisual works, to perform the copyrighted work publicly;
5. in the case of literary, musical, dramatic, and choreographic works, pantomimes, and pictorial, graphic, or sculptural works, including the individual images of a motion picture or other audiovisual work, to display the copyrighted work publicly; and
6. in the case of sound recordings to perform the copyrighted work publicly by means of a digital audio transmission.

The concept is fairly simple in terms of making copies of a work. However, some of the other rights can become a bit complex, particularly in determining what a derivative work is. When a work is recast, transformed, or adapted, it is a derivative work. Translations of works are derivatives. Copyright holders can authorize public use of displays, performances, and distributions of their work, but they have no say in the private use of their works.

The duration of copyright has increased dramatically over the years of the Copyright Act. In the early years, authors had exclusive rights to their works for fourteen years with an option to renew for another fourteen years. For many years duration remained for the life of the author plus fifty years after the author's death. However, in 1998, Congress passed the Sonny Bono Copyright Term Extension Act (CTEA),[13] which added another twenty years of protection. Disney lobbied Congress quite diligently to add more years to protection, since the copyright in one of their most valuable assets, Mickey Mouse, was set to expire. Congress was swayed by Disney's efforts, which resulted in the longer protection of copyrighted works. The constitutionality of the CTEA was challenged in the U.S. Supreme Court in a case called *Eldred v. Ashcroft*.[14] In 2003 Justice Ginsberg delivered the opinion for the Court. The Justices ruled in a 7–2 decision that CTEA was constitutional. Congress has the authority to extend the term of copyright for as many years as they want, provided it is not an unlimited term. Justice Ginsberg cited the Copyright Clause in the Constitution, which states that "Congress shall have the power . . . to promote the Progress of Science and Useful Arts, by securing for limited Times." CTEA survived the challenge. It would not be a surprise if Disney and other content holders were back on Capitol Hill lobbying Congress for further extensions to copyright duration, since the twenty-year extension of protection is almost at an end for some works.

Copyright duration for works published or created in or after 1978 now stands at life of the author plus seventy years or in the case of works for hire such as corporations, the term is either one hundred twenty years from creation of the work or ninety-five years from publication, whichever is shorter. Trying to determine if works published prior to 1978 are still protected can prove quite difficult. Works were required to be registered with the Copyright Office and registration had to be renewed twenty-eight (28) years after publication. If the work was not renewed, then the copyright expired. Until 1989 works also had to have a notice on them.[15] The notice consisted of the word copyright or the copyright symbol ©, the year of publication and the copyright holder's name. If the notice was not included on the work, then the work became part of the public domain. There were changes to the act over the years that allowed copyright holders to correct the errors, which actually makes it even trickier to determine whether or not a work is still protected by copyright. Due to some of the changes in the duration, the duration clock was stopped on works published in the United States prior to January 1, 1923. Their copyright has expired, and they are now in the public domain. The next set of works will enter the public domain on January 1, 2019, and they will be works published in 1923; in 2020 works published in 1924 will enter the public domain, and so on. To assist in unraveling some of the complexities of determining if a work is in the public domain, Peter Hirtle from Cornell University developed a chart[16] that was based in part on Lolly Gasaway's chart[17] on when U.S. works will enter the public domain.

The increasingly longer terms of protection of copyrighted works have resulted in a whole panoply of other issues. As each year passes, more works are becoming orphan works, which are works whereby the copyright owner either cannot be identified or cannot be located. What does a user do when they want to use a copyrighted work because their use falls outside the exceptions granted under the U.S. Copyright Act but they cannot locate the owner of the work to seek permission? There is an inherent risk that should they move forward and use the work, they will be vulnerable to being sued if the copyright owner comes forward and identifies him- or herself. This conundrum is not just faced by academics but by movie studios, photographers, and others who use portions or all of protected works to create new works. In 2005 the U.S. Copyright Office conducted a study and held roundtables to discuss the issue and identify possible solutions. Their 2006 final report[18] was submitted to Congress and legislation was introduced to deal with the issue. It did not pass and was again raised in 2008, but that initiative died as well. Both pieces of proposed legislation incorporated many of the recommendations of the 2006 report. The major thrust was to diminish liability for users of copyrighted works who had made a good faith effort in trying to identify and/or locate the copyright owner. The Copyright Office has taken up the cause once again, and in October 2012, they posted a Notice of Inquiry[19] asking for public comments on how the orphan works environment has changed since the earlier report and how should orphan works be treated in mass digitization projects. In March 2014 they held roundtable discussions on the orphan works issue and mass digitization.[20] The roundtable speakers included representatives from academic libraries and major content holders such as publishers. There was no consensus among the participants, which could make moving forward with orphan works legislation a difficult task. The orphan works issue needs to be addressed so that new works can be created. Many authors are too fearful of potential lawsuits, so they do not incorporate orphan works into their new work.

For copyright holders to sue an alleged infringer, they must show that they have a valid copyright in the work; that the infringer had access to the work; and that the infringer violated one of the exclusive rights of the copyright owner. There can be civil and criminal penalties associated with copyright infringement. If it's a civil action, then the wronged party is asking the court to award them money for the damages they have sustained. Criminal liability results in the infringer potentially going to jail. Individuals and corporations can bring civil actions but only the government can bring a criminal action. Copyright has a three-year statute of limitations for both civil and criminal complaints. A statute of limitations requires that the person claiming the harm, generally referred to as the plaintiff, must file a legal claim within three years of when the infringement occurred. If they do not file a claim within that time, then they lose the right to sue the alleged infringer. If the complaint is filed after the statute of limitations, the court will dismiss it without hearing the merits of the case. There could be an occasion whereby the court might allow the action to proceed if the plaintiff can show that it was unreasonable for them to discover that the infringement had occurred within that three-year time limit.

Infringing someone's copyright can be quite costly. There are money damages that can range from $750 to $150,000 per infringement as determined by the Copyright Act, or the copyright owner can request that the court grant them actual damages and lost profits.[21] Copyright owners can also ask to be reimbursed for attorney's fees and court costs, all of which can be quite hefty. In addition, illegal copies can be impounded and courts can issue injunctions to stop the illegal behavior. In order to reap the full benefit of damages under the Copyright Act, copyright owners should register their copyright with the U.S. Copyright Office. Boston University student Joel Tenenbaum found out the hard way how serious copyright owners and the courts are about enforcing copyright owners' rights. Tenenbaum was sued in 2009 by several recording companies for illegally downloading and sharing thirty songs. After many years of legal wrangling, the First Circuit Court of Appeals in Boston upheld the fine of $22,500 per song for a total of $675,000, finding Tenenbaum's behavior egregious.[22]

In copyright infringement cases there are three types of liability: direct, contributory, and vicarious. Direct infringers are the ones who actually do the infringing. In a contributory infringement claim, the infringer encouraged or assisted in the infringement. Vicarious infringement occurs when the infringer has the authority and ability to supervise the infringement and has a financial interest in it. This is generally the situation in an employer-employee relationship.

The Copyright Act provides some protection to librarians and educators in infringement claims. The law requires that they act in good faith. If the infringer is an employee or agent of a nonprofit educational institution, library, or archives and was acting within the scope of her employment by making copies of the copyrighted work and believed and had reasonable grounds for believing that her use was fair use, then the court is not allowed to assess statutory damages. However, the court can still order payment of actual damages and other remedies.

There are exceptions granted by the Copyright Act, such as fair use and educational use. These exceptions will be discussed in detail in later chapters. However, it is important to note that such exceptions can be complex in their application. What might appear to be a very simple and straightforward fair-use analysis can become bogged down with the intricacies. Specific examples of such applications will be provided in later chapters. We will see how the analysis by a user can differ greatly from a court interpretation.

## NOTES

1. Statute of Anne, 8 Anne, c. 19 (1710), accessed April 10, 2014, http://avalon.law.yale.edu/18th_century/anne_1710.asp.

2. U.S. Const. art. 1, § 8, cl. 8.

3. M. A. Pallante, "The Next Great Copyright Act," *Columbia Journal of Law and the Arts* 36 no. 3 (2013): 315–44, accessed April 10, 2014, http://www.copyright.gov/docs/next_great_copyright_act.pdf.

4. U.S. Copyright Act, 17 U.S.C. § 102(a).

5. Burrow Giles Lithograph Company v. Sarony, 111 U.S. 53 (1884).

6. Bridgeman Art Library, Ltd. v. Corel Corporation, 36 F.Supp2d 191 (1999).

7. Feist Publications, Inc. v. Rural Telephone Service Co., Inc. 499 U.S. 340 (1991).

8. BellSouth Advertising & Publishing Corporation v. Donnelly Information Publishing, Inc., 999 F.2d 1436 (11th Cir. 1993).

9. U.S. Copyright Act, 17 U.S.C. § 102(a).

10. U.S. Copyright Act, 17 U.S.C. § 102(a).

11. U.S. Copyright Act, 17 U.S.C. § 102(b).

12. U.S. Copyright Act, 17 U.S.C. § 106.

13. Sonny Bono Copyright Term Extension Act, Pub. L. 105-298, U.S. Stat. 112 (1998).

14. Eldred v. Ashcroft, 537 U.S. 186 (2003).

15. In 1989 the United States joined the Berne Convention. As part of the requirements to join Berne, the United States had to discontinue the formalities of registration and notice to be in compliance with other Berne member nations.

16. Peter B. Hirtle, *Copyright Term and the Public Domain in the United States: 1 January 2014*, Cornell Copyright Information Center, 2014, accessed April 10, 2014, http://copyright.cornell.edu/resources/publicdomain.cfm.

17. Lolly Gasaway, "When U.S. Works Pass into the Public Domain," University of North Carolina, 2003, accessed April 10, 2014, http://www.unc.edu/~unclng/public-d.htm.

18. United States Copyright Office, *Report on Orphan Works: A Report of the Register of Copyrights* (Washington, DC: Library of Congress, 2006), accessed April 10, 2014, http://www.copyright.gov/orphan/orphan-report.pdf.

19. United States Copyright Office, "Notice of Inquiry, Orphan Works and Mass Digitization," *Federal Register* 77, No. 204 (Monday, October 22, 2012, Notices): 64555, accessed April 10, 2014, http://www.copyright.gov/fedreg/2012/77fr64555 .pdf.

20. Claire Cassedy, "Discussion on Orphan Works and Mass Digitization at U.S. Copyright Office, March 10–11, 2014," *Knowledge Economy International* (March 17, 2014), accessed April 10, 2014, http://keionline.org/node/1978.

21. U.S. Copyright Act, 17 U.S.C. § 504.

22. J. Panzar. "Large Fine Upheld against BU Grad for Illegal Song Downloads," *Boston Globe*, June 27, 2013, accessed August 26, 2013, http://www.bostonglobe. com/metro/2013/06/26/court-upholds-fine-against-former-student-for-illegal-music -downloads/aXul4dPHxzv5mrnDUehaEN/story.html.

# 3

## University Culture

According to the 2013 statistics from the U.S. Department of Education,[1] there were 4,599 degree-granting institutions during the 2010–2011 year in the United States. Over twenty-one million students were enrolled at those institutions during that year. Each institution has their own culture based upon numerous factors such as private vs. public; religious affiliation; small vs. large; geographic location; for-profit vs. nonprofit; Carnegie classification; and the types of majors and disciplines they offer. The diversity of institutions is reflected in their approach to intellectual property issues.

### TECHNOLOGY TRANSFER

At many institutions ownership of copyrighted works is subsumed under a technology transfer office or commercialization office with patents. Patents generally receive top priority since they have the potential to make large sums of money for the university. Technology transfer offices usually manage the university's intellectual property. They are charged with bringing inventions to the market. The following are some of the descriptions of such offices.

*University of Notre Dame, Office of Technology Transfer*:

Assist in the commercialization of University Inventions
Patent, market, and license the products of University Research
Increase the impact of the research endeavors undertaken at Notre Dame
Provide guidance in matters relating to University Intellectual Property[2]

*Harvard University Office of Technology Development (OTD)*:

OTD's mission is to make the fruits of Harvard research more accessible outside the University, including underserved communities, and ensure that society benefits from Harvard innovations by fostering their swift, professional and effective development and commercialization. Our specific objectives include:

Ensuring that Harvard research results are made widely available and trans-formed for public use and benefit.

Serving as a dynamic bridge from laboratory to industry to make certain that promising new technologies are translated into products and services that benefit society and the world.

Evaluating, patenting and licensing inventions and discoveries made by faculty of Harvard University, Harvard Medical School, Harvard School of Public Health and the School of Engineering and Applied Sciences.

Stimulating innovation and technology development within the Harvard com-munity and securing all necessary protection of the resulting intellectual property.

Licensing Harvard technologies to strong, effective partners.

Establishing start up ventures and building value around Harvard innovations.

Building sponsored research collaborations with industry around faculty-initiated applied research projects[3]

*UCLA Office of Intellectual Policy and Industry Sponsored Research*:

OIP-ISR supports UCLA's research, education and service mission by

1. Commercializing intellectual property rights;
2. Facilitating collaborations with industry for next-generation scientific breakthroughs;
3. Advancing UCLA entrepreneurship and research; while
4. Protecting the university's interests by managing risk; and
5. Promoting economic growth in California.

The scope of activities include

1. Commercially evaluating new technologies;
2. Determining patentability and commercial value;
3. Prosecuting patents;
4. Marketing and licensing inventions;
5. Facilitating UCLA faculty startups;
6. Engaging industry to facilitate research collaboration;
7. Negotiating license agreements and Material Transfer Agreements; and
8. Receiving and distributing royalties and other income to the inventors, UCLA Campus and its Departments.[4]

Hamilton College, a small private college in New York, has two policies that address intellectual property issues. The first is their "Policy on the Determination of Ownership of Intellectual Property,"[5] and the second is the "Policy on College-Owned Intellectual Property."[6] The policies are managed by the vice president for academic affairs, unlike larger institutions that have specific intellectual property offices. Some smaller institutions do not have as sophisticated policies and systems as do their larger counterparts, due mostly to the smaller volume of marketable intellectual property. However, Hamilton's policies, particularly their statements on how they will manage what the college owns, is very succinct, specific, and quite comprehensive. The following are excerpts from that policy.

(X) The Office of the VPAA will be responsible for day-to-day management of all College IP issues, and shall be empowered to negotiate the College's rights under this policy and resolve matters described under "deliberative determination." All IP to be disclosed to the College pursuant to this policy shall be disclosed to the Office of the VPAA (the "Office"), which will be responsible for timely review of all disclosures. The Office will complete a review of the patentability and marketability of IP and prepare a recommendation for the VPAA regarding the IP. The Office shall be responsible, working with creators, for obtaining patent, copyright, or other protection of IP owned by the College hereunder, and for marketing and licensing of all such IP rights. The Office shall also set up and manage individual expense and income accounts for IP that is vested in the College under this policy.

(XI) College Personnel who wish to pursue the commercialization of their independently developed and owned IP through the College may offer such intellectual property to the College by disclosing the IP to the Office of the VPAA. The Office will evaluate the commercial potential of the intellectual property and make a recommendation to the VPAA regarding the acceptance of the intellectual property. Acceptance of such IP by the College will be made at the sole discretion of the College and will require creator(s) to accept all provisions of this policy, including the assignment of rights and income distributions.

Note that copyright is not specifically mentioned in many of the above examples. However, copyright can certainly play a part in many of the areas, such as licensing. "Commercializing intellectual property rights" as stated above in the UCLA statement would also include copyrighted works. These examples are an overview of the various approaches by institutions to manage their marketable intellectual property. The practice and scope varies by institution but is very much driven by the institutional culture.

## GENERAL INTELLECTUAL PROPERTY POLICIES

Universities have intellectual property policies that delineate the ownership rights of faculty, staff, and students for patents and copyrights. University trademarks are usually managed by a separate department, but some policies include a statement of ownership in all university trademarks. It is generally the responsibility of the technology transfer departments or research offices to implement the intellectual property policies.

Intellectual property policies run the gamut from the very simple to the complex. They can be policies that specify the rights of employees and the university for the ownership of any works created at the institution, be they copyrights or patents. They can be policies that spell out the responsibilities for using copyrighted works and policies that combine both use and ownership.

## OWNERSHIP POLICIES

Ownership policies generally address copyrights and patents separately within the policy. The patent section specifies the division of royalties and the patent process. The copyright section defines which works will be owned by the faculty and which ones the university will claim an interest in. Generally, the copyright in traditional scholarly and instructional works such as books, journal articles, and classroom materials are retained by the faculty. Such works are defined as follows in Purdue University's Intellectual Property Policy.[7]

> The term "Instructional Copyrightable Work" means a Copyrightable Work that a) is authored by an identifiable University faculty member or instructor primarily for the instruction of students, b) is not specifically commissioned by the University, and c) is not a recording of a teaching performance made to or for University students.
>
> The term "Scholarly Copyrightable Work" means a Copyrightable Work created by any person subject to this policy primarily to express and preserve scholarship as evidence of academic advancement or academic accomplishment. Such works may include, but are not limited to, scholarly publications, journal articles, research bulletins, monographs, books, plays, poems, musical compositions and other works of artistic imagination, and works of students created in the course of their education, such as exams, projects, theses or dissertations, papers and articles.

Copyright in syllabi and online courses might be either owned by the university or shared with the university. For example the following is an excerpt from Georgetown University's Intellectual Property policy regarding nontraditional copyrighted works.

> While the University generally has not sought assignment by Covered Individuals of the copyrights in their traditional scholarly works (written or edited), it has generally required assignment of ownership rights in all other Intellectual Property made or conceived by Covered Individuals utilizing the facilities, equipment, funds or other contributions of the University to a degree that is substantially in excess of what is normally provided to Covered Individuals. Consequently, in cases not involving traditional scholarly works, when the University provides substantially more than the usual support for the creation of copyrightable material or commercially valuable collections of information—for example, by subventing publication of scholarship or by committing University resources for the development of digital materials for teaching and learning—formal arrangements (created at the OTL) must be drafted in order to ensure that rights, responsibilities, and prospective revenues are shared equitably between those who develop the Intellectual Property and the University as the provider of auspices and facilitating resources.[8]

Some policies require disclosure of only copyrighted works that have potential marketable value. In some cases it can be difficult to ascertain whether or not the work would be a good fit for any type of licensing. It is typical in ownership policies to spell out the work-for-hire doctrine so that employees other than faculty are aware that any works they create while employed at the university will be owned by the university unless there is an agreement to the contrary. Some policies will specify that significant use of university funds or resources entitles the university to ownership. University ownership policies also clarify that if the work product is a result of sponsored research or a grant, then the university will take ownership in order to ensure that all obligations under such contracts are met. There are some recent policies that have added a clause that grants universities a nonexclusive license to student theses/dissertations, more than likely in response to open-access initiatives. For example, MIT's intellectual property policy states that within certain parameters students own the copyrights to their theses; "however, a student must, as a condition to a degree award, grant royalty-free permission to the Institute to reproduce and publicly distribute copies of his/her thesis."[9] A good intellectual property policy will also provide a procedure for dispute resolutions.

## USE POLICIES

Policies for use of copyrighted works range from very specific to more general statements. For example, Washington and Lee University has a very detailed copyright use policy, which also incorporates guidelines into it.[10] The introduction to their policy states

> It is the intent of Washington and Lee University that all members of the University community adhere to the provisions of the United States Copyright Law. Each member of the University community must take some individual responsibility for copyright compliance, and these extensive guidelines flow from this premise. Conforming to this policy may in some cases result in additional costs to the student for course materials and some additional inconvenience and time delay in the preparation procedure of those materials. Members of the University community who willfully disregard the copyright policy do so at their own risk and assume all liability.

They provide basic information on fair use but then quite detailed information on acceptable use of photocopying for teaching and research, reserves, interlibrary loan, and guidelines for use of films and videos.

An example of a very general policy is the one from the University System of Georgia, which basically says that they will adhere to the U.S. Copyright Act and provides some fair-use information.[11] It states that

> As a system devoted to providing the highest quality undergraduate and graduate education to students; pursuing leading-edge basic and applied research, scholarly inquiry, and creative endeavors; and bringing intellectual resources to the citizenry, the University System of Georgia is committed to respecting the rights of copyright holders and complying with copyright law. The University System of Georgia recognizes that the exclusive rights of copyright holders are balanced by limitations on those rights under federal copyright law, including the right to make a fair use of copyrighted materials and the right to perform or display works in the course of face-to-face teaching activities.

It continues with descriptions of the steps that they take to inform their constituents about copyright law and their obligation to comply with the law.

Some are not policies as much as guidelines and there are some universities who still follow the 1976 Classroom Guidelines with caveats. For example, Yale University Division of the Vice President and General Counsel issued a discussion page and guidelines for academic copying and course packets that reflect the restrictions of the 1976 Guidelines.[12] Their memorandum begins with the following general statement:

> University policy requires all members of the Yale community to comply with the U.S. Copyright Act and related copyright laws. Respect for intellectual property rights is a shared value of the Yale community. Furthermore, violations of the law can result in liability for substantial damages to the copyright holder (and in extreme cases even criminal penalties).

It continues with specific directives to faculty and staff that they should obtain permission from the copyright holder before making copies for student use unless the use could be considered fair use under the copyright law. They go on to acknowledge that the application of fair use is not an exact science, so the Office of General Counsel should be contacted with specific questions.

Information technology departments also have copyright use policies but generally in tandem with computer use policies. Such policies are usually directed toward students and include a warning that copyright infringement is not allowed on university computers or through the university network. Students have to agree to the terms of use in order to gain access to the network. There can be multiple layers of such agreements with students, particularly if they live in campus housing such as residence halls, which can have their own networks. Employees usually agree to comply with the copyright law as a condition of employment.

Student handbooks can address copyright use as well. This is generally part of honor codes, which dictate acceptable student behavior on campus. The regulations can be fairly general, such as students are to respect copyright and remain in compliance with U.S. law. Some can provide a bit more of basic copyright information but will then refer the student to campus resources for further information.

## RISK MANAGEMENT

Universities are usually quite reluctant to assume a lot of legal risk. Most have risk management departments that will assess the liability to the university should they pursue a certain course of action. The risk analysis certainly does not only address intellectual property issues but anything that can potentially cause harm to the institution. There is a risk associated with a copyright analysis of use of a work. The exceptions, particularly fair use, have quite a bit of flexibility or vagueness in the assessment of the factors. It is a risk to the university should the person or department apply the exceptions incorrectly. To mitigate the risk, an option is to obtain permission to use copyrighted materials, which could certainly include paying royalties for major initiatives or projects such as e-reserves or digitizing dissertations. On the other side of the coin there are universities who have weighed the pros and cons of not backing down from a legal challenge, such as Georgia State University did when publishers challenged the legality of their electronic reserves. Sometimes the long-term benefits can outweigh the short-term risk. The risk analysis from such departments can assist administrators in responding to potential legal issues, but generally it is only one factor to be considered when looking at the larger picture.

## CONCLUSION

What can be confusing at times is the plethora of copyright information from different sources within a university. It's sometimes hard to distinguish whether it is a policy, guideline, or just information. There can be copyright information posted on the following departmental websites: general counsel, copyright office, libraries, technology transfer, office of research, information technology, dean of students office, and various others depending upon the institution. There are some institutions that attempt to have a centralized web page of all copyright resources at the university so users can just click on the links, which should take them to the needed information. Sometimes this can be problematic, however, if the links do not work. Users are then back to square one trying to navigate large university websites that can at times appear to have conflicting information.

Each university has its own culture and environment and the policies reflect this diversity. Policies come in all shapes and sizes and can be a complicated labyrinth to maneuver. It's incumbent upon the employees and the students to be aware of the intellectual property policies at the beginning of any project or initiative so that there are no surprises down the road that can complicate and sometimes derail a project.

## NOTES

1. National Center for Education Statistics, "Table 220: Historical Summary of Faculty, Enrollment, Degrees, and Finances in Degree Granting Institutions: Selected Years, 1869–70 through 2010–11," *Digest of Education Statistics* (Washington, DC: United States Department of Education, 2013), accessed April 10, 2014, http://nces.ed.gov/programs/digest/d12/tables/dt12_220.asp.

2. University of Notre Dame, "Office of Technology Transfer," 2014, accessed April 10, 2014, http://ott.nd.edu/.

3. Harvard University Office of Technology Development, "About Us," 2014, accessed April 9, 2014, http://otd.harvard.edu/about/.

4. University of California, Los Angeles, Office of Intellectual Property and Industry Sponsored Research, "About Us," 2014, accessed April 10, 2014, http://oip.ucla.edu/about-us.

5. Hamilton College, *Policy on the Determination of Ownership of Intellectual Property (IP)* (Clinton, NY: Hamilton College, 2005), accessed April 10, 2014, https://my.hamilton.edu/documents/IP_policy_final_dec20051.pdf.

6. Hamilton College, *Policy on College-Owned Intellectual Property* (Clinton, NY: Hamilton College, 2005), accessed April 10, 2014, https://my.hamilton.edu/documents/IP_policy_collegeowned1.pdf.

7. Purdue University, "Purdue University Policies: Intellectual Property (I.A.I)," 2014, accessed April 10, 2014, http://www.purdue.edu/policies/academic-research-affairs/ia1.html.

8. Georgetown University, *Georgetown University Intellectual Property Policy* (Washington DC: Georgetown University, 2006), accessed April 10, 2014, http://studentaffairs.georgetown.edu/studentaffairs/policies/studentconduct/intellectual property/document/1242777712827/Intellectual-Property-Policy.pdf.

9. Massachusetts Institute of Technology, "Ownership of Intellectual Property," *MIT Policies and Procedures*, accessed April 10, 2014, http://web.mit.edu/policies/13/13.1.html.

10. Washington and Lee University, "Policy for the Use of Copyrighted Works," *Code of Policies*, 2007, accessed April 10, 2014, http://www2.wlu.edu/x30754.xml.

11. University System of Georgia, "Policy on the Use of Copyrighted Works in Education and Research," *USG Copyright Policy*, accessed April 10, 2014, http://www.usg.edu/copyright/.

12. Yale University, Division of the Vice President and General Counsel, "Copyright: Academic Copying and Student Course Packets," 2014, accessed April 10, 2014, http://ogc.yale.edu/copyright-academic-copying-and-student-course-packets.

# 4

## Establishing a Copyright Office

Establishing a copyright office or appointing a copyright officer is something that usually occurs after a great deal of thought and discussion at many levels throughout a university. Budget, space, and staffing of the office as well as the credentials of the copyright officer are only some of the issues that must be decided before the office opens for business.

### PLACEMENT

One of the first questions that needs to be answered is where will the office be housed or where will the copyright officer reside? What is their placement within their organization? Part of that equation is who supervises the office. There are numerous models, but the most common involve housing the office in the libraries or legal counsel office. However, a copyright office can also be part of technology transfer offices, provost offices, or research offices.

Placement of a copyright office can sometimes be equated with how much authority the office has on campus. A study conducted by Rebecca Albitz found that copyright officers that are housed in libraries believed that "they would have more authority if their office were located either under a general counsel's umbrella or in the provost's office."[1] The type of authority the copyright officer will have within the university needs to be addressed when establishing a copyright office. Careful consideration of the implications of placement and how that placement will be perceived is critical.

## STAFFING

Copyright offices generally have a very small staff. Copyright officers need to think outside of the box in looking at staffing options. The following are some questions to take into consideration when determining staffing levels.

1. Will there be additional funding for staffing to support the office? This could be secretarial assistance, students, internships or central administrative support.
2. Will this be dedicated support or will the staff be shared with other departments?
3. Will it be full-time support or part-time support?
4. What level of staffing is needed? This can vary at times depending upon projects undertaken by the office. Hiring students or interns can be a good solution to focus on a specific project. In education there is always a diverse pool of very talented students who are looking more for experience than money, which is a great boon for tight budgets.
5. What skills are required? For a basic secretarial position, general computer skills such as Word, PowerPoint, and Excel would be needed. Copyright officers generally offer many presentations using PowerPoint or something similar. Would there be expectations for staff to actively assist in developing such presentations or would it be more proofreading skills that would be necessary? Many copyright offices have websites. Would the staff person need advanced technical skills to help build the website or only a basic understanding in order to maintain the site? What kind of design skills would be needed, if any? Would they need to help design the website or any publications distributed by the office? If so, then that is whole a different level of qualifications that must be added to a job description. Are they expected to assist with research? If so, then is it only basic research such as locating a journal article or is it more in-depth such as tracking down some legislation or a legal case?
6. What interpersonal skills are needed? Excellent interpersonal skills are critical to a support staff position in a copyright office. Staff generally interact with people from all over the university and beyond. At times, some of the interactions can be a bit tense, so diffusing the situation requires patience, tact, and diplomacy.
7. What kind of training might be needed if staff do not have skills in all the necessary areas? Are there in-house training or staff development programs that they can participate in that are usually free of charge, or will they need to attend programs that have a fee associated with them?

8. If there are multiple staff positions, are there managerial skills that would be required in order to supervise other staff?
9. What credentials are required for a staff position? What level of education and/or experience would be required? Sometimes the minimum qualification would be a high school diploma and two years of secretarial experience. Other times, it could be a college degree that is required. Will years of experience be able to be substituted for any educational requirements?
10. Will staff be required to handle confidential information? If there is a legal component to the office, then understanding and heeding confidentiality requirements is also crucial.

## BUDGETS

Determining a budget for the office can be difficult because of all the unknown expenses. Sometimes salaries and benefits are separate from the office budget, but this is something that should be verified before submitting a draft budget for approval. Either way, salaries and dollar amounts for employee benefits must be factored in to the overall cost of an office. Monies for office supplies need to be added in as well. This can range from thumb drives to printer paper/toner to pens. If this is a brand new office, then this category could also include office furniture such as desks, chairs, bookcases, file cabinets, and a conference table, as well as computer, printer, and scanner. Of course those types of expenses would not be a yearly occurrence.

Expenses for communication might sometimes need to be added into a budget. There are charges for telephones and data connections. Will the university reimburse the copyright officer for use of their personal cell phone for business as well as contributing to the cost of accessing e-mail and the Internet? Or will it be a dedicated phone provided by the university? Are there policies governing the use of the equipment? All need to be considered and added to the bottom line.

Research resources can tend to be pricey unless the expenses are shared. The resources can consist of both print and online sources but should include access to legal services such as Lexis/Nexis or Westlaw. Those databases are generally used by a legal counsel's office or a law school. They are more substantive than the versions that are licensed to university libraries for basic legal research. Many resources are now online, but there are still some works that are print only and should be included in the copyright officer's professional library. Another facet to this budget line is whether or not professional association fees will be paid for by the university and if so, is it included in

## PROFESSIONAL LIBRARY

Crews, Kenneth D. *Copyright Law for Librarians and Educators: Creative Strategies and Practical Solutions*. 3rd Edition. Chicago: American Library Association, 2012.

Epstein, Michael A. *Epstein on Intellectual Property*. 5th Edition. New York: Aspen Publishers, 2014.

Geller, Paul E., and Melville B. Nimmer. *International Copyright Law and Practice*. New York: Matthew Bender & Company, LexisNexis Group, 2013.

Goldstein, Paul. *Goldstein on Copyright*. 3rd Edition. New York: Aspen Publishers, 2014.

LexisNexis legal research database.

Nimmer, Melville B., and David Nimmer. *Nimmer on Copyright*. New York: Matthew Bender & Company, Inc., LexisNexis Group, 2013.

Westlaw legal research database.

research resources or is it a separate budget line? If the copyright officer is an attorney, will the university pay for the annual bar membership fee for their state? Will it also include paying for continuing legal education credits, which are required by some bars? Will they pay for professional development programs for the copyright officer and their staff? All of these fees can add up, so it's good to know how much will be needed to include in the budget.

Will there be funds available for travel? If so, is it one lump sum that is allowed per year or is there flexibility to use what is needed for professional travel? Are there restrictions on what travel money can be used for in terms of types of meetings, programs, and so forth? Some travel costs can be estimated if attendance at annual meetings or organizations is required since they are generally scheduled years in advance of the event. One will know the location and dates of meetings, so a ballpark figure can be calculated for attendance. However, there are programs and meetings that can crop up during the year, so it is good to have a reserve fund to cover the unanticipated costs.

## COPYRIGHT OFFICER CREDENTIALS

The most difficult decision that administrators need to make is determining the necessary credentials for a director of a copyright office or a copyright officer as well as their responsibilities. Will the position be devoted to copyright issues or will the person have other responsibilities as well? If the position is part of the libraries, then other duties such as reviewing and negotiating the library's licensing resources are sometimes combined with providing copyright services.

A trend in libraries is to create a scholarly communications librarian position and have copyright responsibilities subsumed under it. There are differences between a scholarly communication position and a copyright officer position. Scholarly communication is defined by the Association of College and Research Libraries (ACRL) as "the system through which research and other scholarly writings are created, evaluated for quality, disseminated to the scholarly community, and preserved for future use. The system includes both formal means of communication, such as publication in peer-reviewed journals, and informal channels, such as electronic listservs."[2] Many scholarly communication positions are responsible for open access initiatives as well as the institutional repository. Copyright encompasses a far broader role than scholarly communication, although there are certainly aspects of it that include copyright issues. When creating a position that is responsible for copyright, administrators need to be able to distinguish the differences between scholarly communication and copyright and make a determination as to what is really needed for the institution. With tight budgets, it's tempting to merge all responsibilities into one position, but it can be very difficult to fully address all the issues that are part of scholarly communication and copyright. The position description should be explicit as to what areas would receive priority.

Another qualification that needs to be considered is whether or not the position will hold faculty status. At some institutions librarians have a special type of faculty status that only applies to librarians, whereas at other institutions they have the same promotion and tenure requirements as all other faculty within the institution. There can be many different definitions of faculty status and the qualifications that go along with them, but that debate is too long to go into in this book. However, should the position be designated a faculty one, then additional qualifications would be required. Classifying a position as faculty rather than professional/administrative is a strategic move and is dependent upon the responsibilities and authority of the position. If the position is part of a legal counsel's office, then the person usually does not have faculty status.

There are numerous models in current practice of the credentials needed for a copyright position. Professional degrees held by the individual could include a Masters in Library Science (MLS), a law degree (JD), both, or another advanced degree. A recent study[3] conducted of the Committee on Institutional Cooperation (CIC) members,[4] otherwise known as the Big Ten of copyright positions, found that six individuals had an MLS, two had a JD, two had both an MLS and JD, and one had a PhD. There is a group of university intellectual property officers (UIPO) that meets occasionally but discusses copyright issues on a regular basis via a listserv. The majority of members in the group are the copyright officers for their institutions, which are primarily major research universities. As of January 2014, there were forty-four members of the group and approximately 68 percent have a law degree and 38 percent have both a JD and MLS. The UIPO group met at Purdue University in April 2013, and one of the topics of discussion was precisely what credentials were needed for a copyright officer. There was no real consensus, only that university cultures differ and that the position must fit within that culture. Laura Gasaway, a noted copyright authority, stated that "a copyright officer is typically required to hold a law degree, and often also a library degree."[5] The question of credentials is explicitly tied in with the responsibilities and duties of the office as well as how much authority the individual has to speak for the institution. Experience in the field is an important factor as well. There are some individuals whose advanced degrees are neither MLS nor JD but have had many years of studying copyright law and the educational issues associated with it and have been advising their institutions as appropriate. Sometimes the determining factor regarding credentials is the salary. Individuals with a law degree generally command more in salary than someone with a master's degree. Tight budgets can then dictate the path of a copyright office and the credentials of the director.

In addition to educational credentials there are other skills that should be considered when hiring a copyright officer. One of the responsibilities of a copyright officer is to educate the community about copyright. To do this successfully, one must be an effective educator and communicator. Excellent public speaking skills as well as an ability to condense and translate complex legal doctrine into understandable concepts for non-lawyers is critical. Strong interpersonal skills and the ability to truly listen and sift through the extraneous information to ascertain the crux of the issue is also very important. Other skills such as time management and the ability to create a broad array of educational materials are also necessary.

A recent review of jobs posted to the American Library Association, the Association of Research Libraries, and the *Chronicle of Higher Education* websites found eight positions that had copyright responsibilities. One position is specifically for a campus copyright librarian with a required MLS degree or equivalent. The required qualifications for that position include "additional experience or education sufficient to perform the responsibilities of the job."[6] Nowhere in the required or preferred qualifications does it require having any knowledge of copyright, yet the majority of responsibilities are copyright related. This position is also responsible for scholarly communication, developing and maintaining the institutional repository, and reviewing and negotiating licenses for electronic resources. There was a position that was recently advertised in the *Chronicle of Higher Education* for a copyright and licensing librarian. The successful candidate would be the "coordinator and consultant on issues that span copyright, licensing and information policies pertaining to library services and initiatives. . . . The individual is responsible for developing, managing and analyzing intellectual property policies that pertain to the creation, addition, or use of copyrighted or licensed content."[7] A master's degree in library science is required and a JD is preferred. The individual must also have significant experience with copyright and licensing content.

Two positions are for directors of libraries and include having some copyright knowledge. One of the positions requires an MLS and the successful candidate must "ensure compliance with all licensing and copyright laws and regulations"[8] along with a myriad of other responsibilities. The other requires an MLS and prefers a second advanced degree as well as "knowledge of copyright rules and changing copyright requirements and licensing for use of materials in classroom instruction, electronic reserves, interlibrary loan, and web-based course management tools."[9]

There are three positions that have scholarly communication in their job title. The first is an assistant dean for scholarly communication and collection development. Part of the job description states that the individual "promotes alternative publishing models and consults on author rights. Provides support to librarians engaged in activities related to scholarly communication, open access, and copyright."[10] The second position is for a director of scholarly communication whose preferred qualifications include "a strong background in copyright" with responsibilities including serving "as a resource on copyright compliance, fair use and other copyright issues."[11] The third position is for a scholarly communication librarian, where the required qualifications include "demonstrated knowledge of or experience with scholarly communication issues, such as copyright, authors' rights, and open access publishing," and the responsibilities include "advises and educates the campus community about authors' rights, faculty use of copyrighted materials, and other copyright issues related to scholarly communication."[12]

Another position is for a research and education librarian in a health science library. The many duties include "monitors and informs faculty, staff, and students on patterns of research and emerging issues associated with scholarly communication and copyright law."[13]

Pennsylvania State University recently advertised for a copyright officer position at their University Park campus. The position requires a "JD, a relevant master's degree, or terminal professional degree in a field relevant to the responsibilities of the job."[14] The position description states that "The Copyright Officer will be a dynamic, innovative, and service-minded expert on matters of copyright and scholarly communication, supporting the University's mission by developing an outreach, education, and consultation program that will help students and faculty understand how copyright and related concepts affect their work."[15] The Copyright Officer is expected to "coordinate with the Office of General Counsel, Information Technology Services and others to help develop and apply policies for intellectual property in the University."[16]

Over the past few years, there have been several copyright officer position openings that require a law degree, and some have university-wide responsibility for copyright. Nova Southeastern University advertised for a copyright officer and the educational requirement was a JD. They needed "three years of professional experience in copyright, fair use, intellectual property and scholarly communication within a legal office or university setting." The job description for the position stated that "the Copyright Officer is the chief resource and consultant on NSU copyright issues, policy and library initiatives within this area. The Copyright Officer is responsible for the implementation and compliance of NSU copyright policies and for the training of NSU community members. The Copyright Officer coordinates the application of policies to meet the NSU mission and its educational, research, and scholarly communication activities and goals."[17]

The University of Ottawa recently undertook a search for a copyright officer and manager of copyright services, which required a law degree. The job summary stated that "the incumbent is responsible for providing leadership and oversight for a comprehensive copyright management program for the entire University community. Within the changing copyright landscape for Canadian universities, the incumbent will develop and implement a long-term copyright strategy and infrastructure that supports the University's academic enterprise and also protects the legal interests of the University, its employees and students."[18]

This is just a snap shot in time, but it reflects some of the diversity of positions with copyright responsibilities in libraries in higher education.

Copyright officers can be part of a general counsel's office. However, "while university attorneys are there to advise the institution on all legal issues, including copyright, they typically are not able to provide services and assistance to individual faculty and staff."[19] Attorneys in a general counsel's office do not represent an individual's personal interest but the university's. There is also the issue of attorney-client privilege. The privilege requires that all communications between attorney and client be confidential. The question that a general counsel's office grapples with is who is the client? They will represent individuals employed at the university and extend the attorney-client privilege to them, but that is only when the legal issue involves the university. Many times copyright questions are more personal in nature. In such a case attorneys have to distinguish between whether the issue at hand has legal implications for the university or if the issue is more of a personal nature for the employee.

If the individual will be associated with a legal counsel's office, then more than likely they will be required to have a JD as well as a membership in a state bar, since they would be perceived as giving legal advice. There are individuals who graduate from law schools who never take the bar examination. However, in order to practice law, individuals must pass the bar exam in the state in which they intend to practice or be waived in. Attorneys who have been practicing law for a certain number of years in one state can sometimes apply for a bar membership in another state based upon the reciprocity rules of that state and their requirements. It usually involves completing a bar membership application indicating the reason for the waiver. If granted, then the attorney does not have to take the bar exam for that state. Every year attorneys must pay a fee to renew their bar license and to remain in good standing. Some state bars also require attorneys to have a specific number of hours of continuing legal education over a period of time usually ranging from one to three years. Each state is different so one must become familiar with the requirements of that state's bar.

If the copyright officer has a JD but is not officially affiliated with the legal counsel's office, then they provide legal information but not legal advice. This can be an extremely sticky situation, since people who seek the information generally perceive that it is legal advice even though there is usually a written and verbal disclaimer to the contrary.

Professional associations and groups provide excellent opportunities to network and share information on current happenings in the copyright environment. They are also a great resource for querying a group on issues that one might not have previously addressed but is currently working on. The following are some associations or groups that a copyright officer might want to become involved with.

*American Library Association*—ALA represents librarians from all different areas of librarianship such as public, academic, school, and special libraries. ALA has numerous committees that address copyright issues that impact their membership:

- Office of Information Technology Policy (OITP), Copyright Education Subcommittee—provides programs and discussions on copyright issues for librarians.

- International Relations Committee—monitors international library issues including copyright. Participates in international meetings and associations.
- Office of Government Relations—monitors Congressional activity on copyright legislation and advocates for improvements to the copyright law.

*Association of College and Research Libraries*—ACRL is a division of ALA. For many years they had a Copyright Committee but disbanded it in 2012. However, they still have several committees that consider copyright issues:

- Government Relations Committee—composes a legislative agenda of issues that impact research and academic libraries. Promotes legislative action on copyright issues as part of a broader agenda.
- SCHOLCOMM Discussion List—provides a forum for discussion on scholarly communication issues, which includes copyright law and policy.
- Copyright Discussion Group—discusses copyright issues of concern to academic and research librarians.

*Association of Research Libraries (ARL)*—one of their focus areas is on copyright and intellectual property issues. They closely monitor court cases, legislation, and international copyright that will impact their members. They also advocate for copyright changes that will benefit their constituencies.

*American Bar Association (ABA)*—Intellectual Property Law Section—Copyright Division—membership is primarily comprised of attorneys who specialize or have an interest in intellectual property. The Copyright Division allows members of the IPL section to focus on copyright in practice.

*National Association of College and University Attorneys (NACUA)*—an organization specifically for attorneys and administrators in higher education.

*Copyright Society of the U.S.A.*—an organization of copyright professionals. Many of the major content holders are well represented. Provides good insight into the practical application of copyright law in the private sector.

*Educause*—an organization of information technology professionals in higher education. Good resource for analysis of trending issues and the copyright impact on them.

This is not an exhaustive listing but these are organizations that provide a good introduction and support for the position.

## ADDITIONAL CONSIDERATION

Universities that have multiple campuses must also determine if the copyright office/officer will be a resource for all campuses, just a few, or only one. Many times this decision will rest on the administrative and legal structure of the university. However, if the copyright officer is responsible for all campuses, then developing a cohesive flow of communication among campuses is quite important. One option is to appoint copyright liaisons at the various campuses that report to the copyright officer. The liaisons can be the go to copyright person on their campus and respond quickly to basic informational needs while discussing and forwarding the more complex questions to the copyright officer for resolution.

Another option is outsourcing copyright services. A company called "Copyright Officer on Call"[20] has recently been developed by attorney Gretchen McCord. McCord provides copyright education and legal advice on copyright issues on a fee basis specifically targeting educational institutions, including K–12 schools. There is a tiered layer of fees for her service, which is divided into hours spent on providing legal information or legal advice as well as fees for training. This new model can certainly be attractive to smaller educational institutions and ones that cannot afford the costs of a copyright office or officer, as well as legal counsel offices that do not have copyright expertise on staff. However, although this service might be beneficial in some situations, a word of caution is needed. There is no substitute for having a copyright expert on campus who understands the culture and can develop on-going relationships with the campus constituencies. Another issue to consider is that there can be complications with providing legal advice, which is tantamount to practicing law if the person is not licensed to practice in that state. It's always good to evaluate options, but educational institutions must not be shortsighted and need to consider the long-term consequences of outsourcing a valuable service such as copyright expertise.

## CONCLUSION

There are many factors that need to be taken into consideration when establishing a copyright office. The credentials, authority, and placement of the copyright officer are the top priorities and will determine the commitment the university has to addressing campus copyright concerns.

## NOTES

1. Rebecca S. Albitz, "Copyright Information Management and the University Library: Staffing, Organizational Placement and Authority," *Journal of Academic Librarianship* 39 (2013): 429–35.

2. Association of College and Research Libraries, Scholarly Communications Committee, "Principles and Strategies for the Reform of Scholarly Communication 1," 2003, http://www.ala.org/acrl/publications/whitepapers/principlesstrategies.

3. Albitz, "Copyright Information Management and the University Library," 429–35.

4. The universities in the study included University of Chicago, University of Illinois–Champaign-Urbana, Indiana University, University of Iowa, University of Minnesota, University of Nebraska–Lincoln, Northwestern University, Ohio State University, Purdue University, and University of Wisconsin–Madison.

5. Laura N. Gasaway, *Copyright Questions and Answers for Information Professionals: From the Columns of Against the Grain* (West Lafayette, IN: Purdue University Press, 2013), 242.

6. American Library Association, "Campus Copyright Librarian, John F. Reed Library, Fort Lewis College," *JobLIST*, accessed January 13, 2014, http://joblist.ala.org/modules/jobseeker/Campus-Copyright-Librarian/24968.cfm.

7. "University of Notre Dame, Copyright and Licensing Librarian," *Chronicle of Higher Education*, accessed February 11, 2014, https://chroniclevitae.com/jobs/0000819098-01.

8. American Library Association, "Manhattan College, Director, O'Malley Library," *JobLIST*, accessed January 13, 2014, http://joblist.ala.org/modules/jobseeker/Director--OMalley-Library/24780.cfm.

9. American Library Association, "Texas A&M University–Corpus Christi, Director, Mary and Jeff Bell Library," *JobLIST*, accessed January 13, 2014, http://joblist.ala.org/modules/jobseeker/Director-Mary-and-Jeff-Bell-Library/24755.cfm.

10. Association of Research Libraries, "Colorado State University Morgan Library, Assistant Dean for Scholarly Communions and Collection Development," *Association of Research Libraries*, accessed January 7, 2014, http://www.arl.org/leadership-recruitment/job-listings/record/a0Id000000CHrkUEAT.

11. American Library Association, "University of Texas at Arlington Libraries, Director of Scholarly Communication," *JobLIST*, accessed January 13, 2014, http://joblist.ala.org/modules/jobseeker/Director-of-Scholarly-Communication/24917.cfm.

12. American Library Association, "Western Washington University, Scholarly Communications Librarian," *JobLIST*, accessed January 13, 2014. http://joblist.ala.org/modules/jobseeker/Scholarly-Communications-Librarian/24759.cfm.

13. American Library Association, "The Ohio State University Health Sciences Library, Research and Education Librarian," *JobLIST*, accessed January 13, 2014, http://joblist.ala.org/modules/jobseeker/Research-and-Education-Librarian-/24942.cfm.

14. Pennsylvania State University, "Copyright Officer, University Park," Accessed April 10, 2014, https://www.libraries.psu.edu/psul/jobs/facjobs/copy.html.

15. Pennsylvania State University, "Copyright Officer, University Park."

16. Pennsylvania State University, "Copyright Officer, University Park."

17. Florida Department of State, Division of Library & Information Services, "Copyright Officer (Attorney)," *Nova Southeastern University*, accessed April 10, 2014, http://www.floridalibraryjobs.org/index.cfm?fuseaction=job .view&jobID=4440&.

18. University of Ottawa, "Copyright Officer, Manager of Copyright Services," *Careers and Jobs*, accessed April 10, 2014, https://client.njoyn.com/CL2/xweb/ Xweb.asp?tbtoken=YF9bRhoXCGgHZ3ACMCZUCCA7AWREcCJUB0ggUFoME 2VfLzUTK0YSBhNxcAkbVhJSQXEqWA percent3D percent3D&chk=dFlbQBJe& clid=27081&Page=jobdetails&jobid=J0113-0072.

19. Gasaway, *Copyright Questions and Answers for Information Professionals*, 242.

20. Gretchen McCord, *Gretchen McCord: Copyright Officer on Call*, accessed April 9, 2014, http://www.copyrightofficeroncall.com.

# 5

## Role of a Copyright Office

Copyright services and the role of a copyright office can take many different directions based upon the needs of the institution and the institution's expectations of the copyright officer. As discussed in a previous chapter, each institution has its own culture, so the provision of copyright services is ruled by that stricture.

### OVERVIEW OF COPYRIGHT
### SERVICES AT COLLEGES AND UNIVERSITIES

Copyright services can take many different forms at universities. Sometimes they are formal positions and other times they are somewhat self-appointed roles. The range of services provided can vary widely as well.

A typical scenario is the assignment of copyright duties to a librarian. This assignment is usually an internal one from libraries administration. It is not something that is university based but more library based, and it is usually not recognized as encompassing the role of an official spokesperson for the university on the topic. This is generally only one responsibility among many. The individual might have expressed an interest in the subject or might have taken some professional development courses in copyright. Some have taken on the role of copyright expert out of necessity or could be in a position in an area such as interlibrary loan, reserves, scholarly communication, or licensing of electronic resources that requires them to have some basic knowledge of copyright. Librarians become the de facto copyright experts on campus due to their reputation as information experts and their dealings with copyright in their profession. However, many librarians are concerned that they will be seen as giving legal advice and do not want to put themselves or their institutions at risk of being sued. They walk a fine line in providing legal information, not legal advice, similar to the dilemma that medical librarians face when confronted with medical questions from patrons. The official assignment of copyright responsibilities to a librarian is increasing but is very diverse. There is no one model that all libraries subscribe to, so it can be difficult to ferret out the person who has that responsibility.

Dedicating a person full-time to providing copyright information at a university-wide level is becoming increasingly more popular as universities grapple with the complex issue of copyright. The first such position that was established at a university was the creation of the Copyright Management Center (CMC) at the Indiana University–Purdue University Indianapolis campus in 1994.[1] The director of the center was Dr. Kenneth Crews, a noted international authority on copyright. The CMC was the prototype for the development of future copyright offices at higher education institutions around the country.

In the late 1990s the CMC was the only stand-alone copyright office. However, there were several pioneers in the field that were recognized copyright experts for higher education and libraries. Georgia Harper from the University of Texas in the General Counsel's Office specialized in intellectual property and copyright for the University. She developed the well-known Copyright Crash Course.[2] Lolly Gasaway was director of the Law Library at the University of North Carolina at Chapel Hill. She is a very well-respected authority on the application of copyright in higher education. She created a comprehensive chart of when works enter the public domain.[3] Peggy Hoon was specializing in copyright at Washington State University before transitioning to a broader role at North Carolina State University, where she developed the TEACH toolkit,[4] which is an invaluable resource.

Purdue University established their copyright office in 2000. The director is "responsible for establishing and leading a University Copyright Office designed to facilitate institutional practices that support the University's research, teaching and service mission through compliance with copyright law, including exercise of the exemptions accorded to users of copyrighted works. Develops and delivers a systematic and ongoing program of copyright education and awareness suitable to the rapidly changing technological and legal environments of higher education."[5]

The Copyright Licensing Office at Brigham Young University "supports the academic and religious mission of Brigham Young University by (1) providing copyright education, training and policy advisement; (2) assuring effective and appropriate copyright/licensing practices; (3) organizing licensing/rights information in a central location; and (4) assessing national/international copyright policy and legal developments. These efforts are coordinated with the University's Office of the General Counsel."[6]

Since 2005 Duke University's Office of Copyright and Scholarly Communications has been responsible for "advising members on legal, technical, copyright and publishing issues; Answering questions about how to best publish and share scholarship; Promoting new models of scholarly communication based on changing technologies and practices, including open access publishing and innovative communications platforms; and Advocating on behalf of Duke and the scholarly community through involvement in national initiatives on copyright and scholarly communications."[7]

The Copyright Advisory Office at Columbia University was founded in 2008 but is currently on hiatus due to the departure of its director, Kenneth Crews. However, the mission of the office is "to address, in a creative and constructive manner, the relationship between copyright law and the work of the university in order to best promote research, teaching, library services, and community involvement." The office "addresses issues of fair use, copyright ownership, and publishing arrangements in furtherance of higher education and the advancement of knowledge; Provides copyright information and education resources for the academic community; Supports innovative policies and practices to foster the creation, preservation, and accessibility of information resources; and Undertakes research and exploration of copyright issues to provide supportive understandings of the law and its importance to educational institutions and libraries."[8]

In 2013 Harvard University created a new position of copyright advisor, which is housed in the Office for Scholarly Communication. The advisor works closely with the general counsel's office and the Harvard Library "to establish a culture of shared understanding of copyright issues among Harvard staff, faculty and students."[9]

However, even with the examples above there is no cookie-cutter approach to the development of such offices or positions. There are many universities that have identifiable copyright offices and officers, but there are many more where the copyright responsibilities are only one part of a person's position or the responsibilities are scattered across the campus. Thus, it is difficult if not impossible to obtain an accurate number of people who provide such services.

There are institutions that have both a copyright office and a general counsel office. Sometimes there is no official affiliation between the two. This can be problematic if there is not a good working relationship between the two offices. A legal counsel office should generally work in tandem with the copyright office if they are separate offices. Much of the relationship depends upon the authority the copyright officer has to provide legal advice, not just legal information. What needs to be established from the very beginning is the role and authority that each has on campus. Generally, copy-right offices have an educational role on campus and also have a broader range of constituents. They are seen as educators and information providers rather than as compliance officers, which can also be referred to as the copy-right police. Legal counsel offices must address only the specific legal issues that are raised, all the while keeping in mind that the client is the university, and not necessarily the individual that seeks answers to their questions. Copy-right officers are not, then, in the position of representing the best interests of the university in the same way that a legal counsel is, and they can be more comprehensive in looking at individual situations and options.

Many times attorneys in legal counsel offices are not all that well versed in copyright law. They might have a nodding acquaintance with it but have many other areas of responsibility. If the copyright officer is not part of the legal counsel's office or associated with it at some level, then there can be potential conflict with the stance on the issues that each office might take.

Another critical issue that can occur is trying to define the distinction between legal information and legal advice. Copyright officers without a law degree can only provide legal information, which in some cases is their interpretation and application of the copyright law. As indicated in the previous chapter, there are some exceptional individuals who do not have a law degree but who have studied copyright for many years and have a very good understanding of it. However, copyright officers who have a law degree can grasp the subtle nuances that arise in all areas of law. Those with a legal back-ground are also trained to recognize the tangential legal areas that can attach to copyright issues, such as trademark, contract, right of publicity, and probate, just to name a few. The flip side, of course, is that attorneys who specialize in copyright law are seen as providing legal advice, not just information. In some cases this could be a correct assumption if the copyright officer is part of the legal counsel's office or if they have been given the authority by their institution to offer such advice. The conundrum happens when copyright officers straddle both worlds. They can have authority to provide legal advice when warranted but otherwise only provide legal information to assist individuals in making an informed decision. The role of the copyright office must be defined before the doors ever open for business. It can certainly change over time as the office evolves and changes occur at the university, but there needs to be a common understanding and agreement among all the players at the outset.

Another decision that must be made prior to the opening of the office is determining who can partake of the services offered by the copyright officer. Primarily, services are provided to faculty and staff of the institution but not necessarily to students, at least on an individual basis. Faculty and staff are employees of the institution and as such the employer has a legal responsibility to them. If employees break the law while they are doing their job, then the institution can be held liable for their actions. Students, on the other hand, have a different legal relationship with the institution. Depending upon the situation, the institution is generally not liable for students' actions such as copyright infringement. There are certainly exceptions where a copyright officer will provide consultations to individual students, but the focus with students is usually at a macro level and providing them with educational materials on copyright. There can certainly be other groups that request access to the services provided by the copyright office, such as alumni, donors, citizens in the town/city/state, and those with a quasi-legal relationship with the university like research partners. There will always be people who request advice and assistance, but that doesn't necessarily mean that they are entitled to it. The scope of clients should be decided early on.

The role of a copyright office is generally multifaceted. The duties and responsibilities are based upon the needs and expectations of the university as well as the credentials of the copyright officer. "The duties of a copyright officer may include the following: (1) developing educational materials, online instruction, and websites about copyright for the institution; (2) offering copyright education and training programs for faculty, students, and staff; (3) assisting the library by reviewing licenses for copyrighted materials; (4) answering questions for individual faculty members about the use of copyrighted works in their teaching and scholarship; (5) advising faculty about copyright transfers for their publications; (6) coordinating activities with the campus office of legal counsel; (7) participating in policy development; and (8) serving as an ex officio member of the campus copyright committee."[10] A study by Albitz also found position responsibilities to include having "some input into general and specific directions their institutions take in implementing the law based upon new court rulings and best practices" as well as "to advocate for the broadest, most liberal definition of copyright in order to support teaching, learning and research."[11] Another potential aspect of the position is ensuring campus compliance with the copyright law.

The provision of copyright information to the university community can take numerous forms. Before embarking on the creation of any educational materials, an environmental scan should be conducted to determine the needs of the campus. One of the most popular educational and marketing tools is a website. Websites are always well received and they can also reach a larger audience than traditional print publications. However, many decisions need to be made before designing a website.

1. What is the purpose of the website?
2. Who is the intended audience for the site?

3. One will also need to consider what resources are available to design, maintain, and update the website. Will the website be a static one or will it be constantly updated with news feeds, additional sections, and frequently asked questions?
4. Will it have an interactive component such as a game, a test, or a sample copyright analysis?
5. Who will monitor the website and make changes as needed?
6. The structure and design of a site can be challenging. Are there requirements imposed by the university in terms of colors and fonts that must be used or conversely not used?
7. Are there standards that must be adhered to for different electronic devices?
8. Are there other departments on campus that provide copyright information?
9. Will this website be the central resource and authority on copyright information for the university?

There is a lot of planning and thought that needs to go into the implementation of a website.

Print publications are also quite popular. They are easy to distribute to individuals and groups and can focus on a specific area of the copyright law such as fair use. The Purdue University Copyright Office has four publications that are used for various purposes. There is a general copyright brochure, which provides highlights of the copyright law related to education and is distributed to all faculty and staff on all campuses at the beginning of the fall semester. Before one can avail oneself of the Technology, Education and Copyright Harmonization Act (TEACH), which is discussed in detail in later chapters, one must meet the requirement of providing "informational materials to faculty, students, and relevant staff members that accurately describe, and promote compliance with, the laws of the United States relating to copyright."[12] The distribution of this brochure would certainly meet this requirement. A second brochure on author rights is provided to many faculty and graduate students during the spring semester. The third publication is entitled "Copyright Law: Your College Career and Beyond." This is a one-page document that is geared toward students and distributed to them when the copyright officer is a guest lecturer or when requested by faculty. It is a succinct overview of how the copyright law applies to students during the course of their college career and also what they should know when they move on to a career. The final publication was developed after consultations with library liaisons who struggled to adequately explain copyright when they spoke to classes in their discipline. It emphasizes talking points for the librarians. Many copyright offices have assorted publications and websites focused on the needs of their clientele.

A website and print publications are one method of educating the campus. However, it is more of a general education. Another way is to provide targeted educational opportunities. This can occur in a variety of ways. It can be as a guest lecturer for undergraduate and graduate courses at the invitation of disciplinary faculty, as a guest at departmental faculty meetings, hosting university-wide workshops on specific aspects of the copyright law, and partnering with campus organizations and nonacademic departments to participate in their events. These can be formal presentations using PowerPoint or similar software or informal presentations. It can also be done as part of a panel or just engaging the audience in a question-and-answer session. The goal is to take advantage of every opportunity presented as well as initiate other ones so that the office is well represented and the campus can identify where to find copyright information.

Another area in which much time is spent by a copyright officer is with individual consultations. Depending upon the scope of the position, this can involve providing information to the entire campus or a smaller defined subset of that. The general topics can range from using copyrighted works in a classroom or for hybrid courses to using works for research to investigating copyright status for digitization projects. You never know what topic you will have to address when someone walks through the door, e-mails you, or is on the other end of the telephone. Usually the issue is far more complex than the client initially discloses. Whether the copyright officer is providing legal information, legal advice, or both, it is in the best interest of all parties to have that clarified right from the initial meeting. I prefer to take copious notes of any meeting where I foresee that there will be further questions, participation, or legal action. I find it useful to have a paper trail of the conversations, since many times a follow-up does not occur for weeks or months. There are times when the issue under discussion also involves other people on campus and/or other areas of law. For example, copyright questions surrounding a donor's gift to the university can also involve contracts, trademarks, estate plans, and rights of privacy and publicity. It helps to include all the players so that the issue is properly addressed.

An approach to take in the initial consultation with the client is to gather as much information as possible and then to conduct a copyright analysis and assess all the options. One of the responsibilities is to not just provide answers to the questions but to have the client participate in the critical thinking and problem solving. The goal is to have them understand how to apply the law to their situation so that they will hopefully be able to resolve similar issues on their own.

An area of consultations that has dramatically increased in recent years is the review of publishing contracts or author agreements. As open-access initiatives become more prevalent, there is greater concern among faculty and graduate students about the rights they need to retain in their works in order to advance their careers and research. Retention of copyright by the author is always the preferred model. However, that is not always possible if the author wants their work published. Discussions with faculty and graduate students around this issue generally involve encouraging them to articulate what types of uses they would need to make of their work and then have them try to negotiate those rights with the publisher. For example, are they bound by open-access policies that require them to place a version of their work in their institutional repository? Is the work the result of a grant that dictates ownership, embargoes, or deposit in a federal government repository like PubMed Central? The copyright officer needs to determine if there are any restrictions that the author is bound by that would prevent compliance with all the terms of the contract. Other clauses in the publishing contract that usually require conversations and explanations include providing the publisher with first option on future works and agreeing to not publish similar works that would compete with the submitted work. Those kinds of clauses are the most contentious and require careful consideration.

Whether it's an open-access policy, an intellectual property policy, or a copyright policy, the copyright officer should be involved in the discussions and drafting of the documents. Copyright officers have unique perspectives, since they interact with people at all levels of the university and have a very good understanding of the issues and concerns as well as the obstacles. Many times policies beget policies in an attempt to address every possible scenario. When this happens there can be a conflict among policies, so having the copyright officer participate on policy committees can help avoid the duplication and confusion.

As discussed in the previous chapter, copyright policies can address either use or ownership or both. If there is no policy on the books, starting from scratch can be daunting. If the copyright officer can lead the effort, all the better. However, if that's not possible, then the copyright officer should be front and center on any policy addressing copyright on campus. It's important to develop a strategy and an approach to crafting the document. The following are some questions that should be considered.

1. What kind of policy is needed—ownership, use, or a combination of both?
2. Who should be involved in drafting a policy? There should be a representative from all the stakeholder groups such as faculty, staff, stu-

dents, librarians, legal counsel, technology transfer, and members of the policy-drafting group.

3. When is the appropriate time to draft a copyright policy? The sooner the better, so that everyone is on the same page.

4. What is the best way to begin in developing a policy? One of the first things to do that is usually very helpful is to do an environmental scan of the institution. This includes looking at what the needs of the institution are in terms of copyright and other intellectual property. Issues must be identified and defined. The current policy, if there is one, needs to be evaluated to see what works, what doesn't, and what has changed, both subject-wise and university-wise, since the inception of the policy. One must also take into account the institutional culture and make sure that any policy aligns well with that.

5. After doing an environmental scan, what would be some of the next steps? The first, as indicated above, is to determine the policy type. Once that is determined it is also very helpful to review other policies from peer institutions or other institutions that have similar cultures or issues. Identify leaders throughout the university that can help advise and seek partnerships with groups on campus that will be impacted by the policy.

Once the policy has been developed, it's important to market the policy so that the individuals that have copyright issues are aware of it. Making campus-wide announcements about the new policy as well as holding forums or Q&A sessions can be helpful. It's important to understand that no policy is perfect and that it is not set in stone. It needs to be reviewed every few years or so to see if it is still relevant and if changes are needed due to shifts in the environment. Copyright litigation involving higher education appears to be increasing, so monitoring developments and impact on copyright policies becomes quite important.

As described in the previous chapter, some copyright officer positions also include assisting the library in reviewing licenses for the acquisition of electronic content. In addition to reviewing the licenses, the individual might also be responsible for negotiating changes and drafting the revisions. This can be an incredibly time-consuming process, especially for large libraries that have a multitude of licenses ranging from the simple to the complex.

The copyright officer can also be charged with obtaining permissions for the use of copyrighted material. The permission process can happen in a variety of ways. It can be permissions for teaching materials including course packs, publications of research materials, digitization projects, grants, and campus performances of music and plays. It can be establishing an account with the Copyright Clearance Center, directly contacting copyright holders, as well as verifying that works are included in the catalogs of performance and music rights agencies that the university might have contracts with, such as ASCAP, BMI, and the Harry Fox Agency. The permissions process can be decentralized in some institutions where faculty, students, libraries, and printing services are responsible for obtaining their own permissions. In other institutions it can be centralized with a copyright office or it can be split, with faculty and students obtaining their own permissions and the copyright office being responsible for departmental permissions.

Many times a campus can have a copyright or intellectual property committee. This committee can be charged with determining the marketability of copyrighted works created at the institution as well as investigating and resolving copyright disputes. Some committees can have an educational component that provides input to the copyright officer about campus copyright issues and needs. It can be a university-wide group, a library-based group, or a group organized by the copyright officer to advise on the direction of the copyright office. Whatever the composition of the committee, the copyright officer should play a role, even as an ex officio member.

Copyright officers have an expertise that is seldom duplicated across campus. Therefore, one of their responsibilities is to monitor copyright legislation and court cases to determine if there would be an impact on their campus. Depending upon the scope of their responsibilities and authority, they could be charged with leading the efforts to make necessary changes in order for the university to be in compliance with the new law and/or court ruling. For example, when the Technology, Education, and Copyright Harmonization Act (TEACH) of 2002[13] went into effect, universities had to meet many requirements in order to take advantage of the new law. The copyright officers were leaders across campus in educating the administrators and faculty about the requirements and structuring the necessary changes. The same is true when a court case is decided, particularly those by the U.S. Supreme Court. If their ruling impacts higher education, then the copyright officer needs to be aware of the specific aspects of the ruling that will require action by the university.

Advocacy is also part of the responsibilities of copyright officers. They advocate on their campuses for the broadest possible interpretation of the copyright law in order to facilitate teaching and research. An example of this is the open-access initiative, which is one of the many areas in which copyright officers advocate for the retention of copyright by researchers. In many ways it began as a grassroots campaign that has taken wings after researchers, universities, and the federal government understood the benefits it could bring to society. In addition, copyright officers participate in legislative hearings and public roundtables hosted by the U.S. Copyright Office and submit comments for the DMCA triennial rulemaking proceedings, which are all on the national level. They also are members and leaders of library and legal committees and associations that address copyright issues within the professional communities.

It is a good idea to maintain statistics on the number of consultations the copyright officer provides over the course of a year as well as the topics covered. It is difficult to count with 100 percent certainty, but it does assist in giving the copyright officer a fairly accurate accounting of his or her time. It is also beneficial in identifying trends in copyright questions and issues. It allows the copyright officer to make adjustments in priorities, which can also impact budgets and staffing.

## CONCLUSION

The role of the copyright office certainly shifts and changes over time. What doesn't change is the need for a copyright expert on campus. As noted above, this can take various forms with many different responsibilities, but the core requirement of providing accurate and timely copyright information and advice remains the same. In fact, the demand for such services is ever increasing as indicated by the growth of such offices over the past fifteen years.

## NOTES

1. Kenneth D. Crews, "The Copyright Management Center at IUPUI: Brief History, Dynamic Changes, and Future Demands," *Indiana Libraries: Journal of the Indiana Library Federation & the Indiana State Library* 19 (1 November 2000): 13–15.

2. Georgia K. Harper, "Copyright Crash Course," University of Texas at Austin, 2007, accessed April 10, 2014, http://copyright.lib.utexas.edu/.

3. Lolly Gasaway, "When U.S. Works Pass into the Public Domain," University of North Carolina, 2003, accessed April 10, 2014, http://www.unc.edu/~unclng/public-d.htm.

4. Peggy Hoon, "The Original TEACH Act Toolkit," J. Murrey Atkins Library, University of North Carolina at Charlotte, 2003, accessed April 10, 2014, http://copyright.uncc.edu/copyright/TEACH.

5. Purdue University Libraries, "Director, University Copyright Office," *Chronicle of Higher Education*, accessed September 9, 1999, http://chronicle.com/free/jobs/admin/legal/12145.html.

6. Brigham Young University, "About Us," BYU Copyright Licensing Office, 2014, accessed April 10, 2014, http://lib.byu.edu/sites/copyright/about/.

7. Duke University, "Office of Copyright and Scholarly Communications," Duke University Libraries, 2013, accessed April 10, 2014, http://library.duke.edu/about/depts/scholcomm.

8. Kenneth D. Crews, "Copyright, Fair Use, and Education," Columbia University Copyright Advisory Office, 2014, accessed April 10, 2014, http://copyright.columbia.edu/copyright/.

9. Harvard University, "Office for Scholarly Communication: OSC Staff," Harvard University Library, 2014, accessed April 10, 2014, https://osc.hul.harvard.edu/osc-staff.

10. Laura N. Gasaway, *Copyright Questions and Answers for Information Professionals: From the Columns of Against the Grain* (West Lafayette, IN: Purdue University Press, 2013), 242.

11. Rebecca S. Albitz, "Copyright Information Management and the University Library: Staffing, Organizational Placement and Authority," *The Journal of Academic Librarianship* 39 (2013): 429–35.

12. U.S. Copyright Act, 17 U.S.C. § 110(2)(D)(i).

13. Technology, Education and Copyright Harmonization Act, Public Law 107-273, Stat. 116 (2002), codified at 17 U.S.C. §§ 110(2) and 112(f).

# 6

## Copyright Services for Librarians

Libraries face a whole host of copyright issues on a daily basis. It can run the gamut from digitization issues in archives and special collections to e-reserves to open-access initiatives. Increasingly, the online environment poses challenges that libraries have not had to deal with before. It is no longer just providing a physical copy of something to loan to a patron but access to works that might be born digital or have no paper counterpart. Librarians navigate the copyright maze attempting to apply what can sometimes appear to be an archaic law to real-life situations. This chapter will identify library issues and pose questions that should be considered when encountering the situation.

### SECTION 108

Section 108 of the U.S. Copyright Act[1] is the exception for libraries and archives. It allows them to make copies of works in their collections under certain circumstances. This section dictates interlibrary loan services, preservation services, and making copies of works for private study. However, before a library can avail itself of the benefits under this exception, it must meet certain requirements.

The first requirement is that the library must be open to the public or the collections must be available to researchers in a specialized field that are not part of the institution the library or archives is associated with. Most academic libraries have no problem meeting this requirement.

The second requirement is that the copy that the library makes or distributes has no direct or indirect commercial advantage. There are some libraries that provide commercial document delivery services to corporations. Copies made for those purposes would not be eligible for the library exception.

The third requirement is that the copy must include a notice of copyright. Many times libraries will include a copy of the page that has the copyright notice on it in addition to the requested copy in order to meet this requirement. If the work does not have a copyright notice, then the copy must include "a legend stating that the work may be protected by copyright."[2] Many libraries have stamps that say "This material may be protected by U.S. Copyright Law" or something similar.

The final requirement is that libraries may only make single copies of works except in very narrow circumstances. The exception does not allow them to make multiple copies for the same individual, nor does it allow for systematic copying of materials. At issue here is a library that has a small budget and tries to avoid purchasing a copy of a journal by having another library make copies of each issue for them.

Libraries are allowed to make copies of works for private study. This could entail making a copy of a book chapter, journal article, or small portion of a larger work, but only under certain conditions. The copy must become the property of the user. The library has no knowledge that said copy would be used for anything other than private study, scholarship, or research. It is not incumbent upon the library to query patrons as to the use of the work they request. However, if the patron indicates that the use of the work is for other than what the law allows, then the library's action would not be protected by section 108. The library must also prominently display where orders are accepted and on the order form a warning of copyright. If a user wants a substantial portion of a work copied or even an entire work, then an additional requirement applies. The library must conduct a reasonable investigation to determine if a copy can be purchased at a fair price. The language in this section is very precise. It only asks that the library make a "reasonable investigation" to obtain a copy at a "fair price." The library does not have to exhaust every avenue looking for a copy, nor does it have to pay an exorbitant amount to obtain the work.

The service of interlibrary loan (ILL) is sanctioned under this section of the U.S. Copyright Act. Libraries can borrow materials from other libraries and also loan materials from their own collections. Many times this is an electronic copy of a journal article or a physical copy of a book. ILL departments must comply with the requirements for private study noted above but also must not engage in borrowing materials for individuals who are trying to circumvent purchasing the work. ILL staff struggle with trying to determine how much is too much to copy or request be copied, since this section is vague. To assist with this dilemma in 1979 the National Commission on

New Technological Uses of Copyrighted Works (CONTU), which had been established by Congress, issued its final report.[3] They provided guidelines for journal articles. They arrived at the magic numbers of allowing a library to borrow up to five copies of an article from the most recent five years of a journal title during one calendar year. This limit is not per patron but per journal title. It is commonly known in the industry as the "rule of five." Many libraries mistakenly believe that this is the law and not just suggested guidelines. It is understandable for library administration to have a finite number for staff to follow. However, the guidelines are not the law and following them could potentially be limiting the scope of ILL requests.

Libraries are allowed to make copies of many categories of copyrighted materials for private study and interlibrary loan. However, there are also some broad restrictions as well. Libraries cannot make copies of motion pictures or other audiovisual works; pictorial, graphic, and sculptural works; and musical compositions. There are some exceptions to these restrictions. Pictures or graphics that are "published as illustrations, diagrams, or similar adjuncts"[4] to works may be copied. For example, a medical journal article that has images of a procedure that accompany the text would not have to be blocked or removed when making a copy of the journal article. Audiovisual works dealing with news may be copied, such as a video clip of a news program, but not a movie that depicts the news industry. Also, musical works are not allowed to be copied.

Section 108 allows for copies to be made for preservation and replacement once a library meets the general qualification listed above. There are different rules that libraries must apply in this situation. The law distinguishes between published and unpublished works.

If a work is published, then a library can make up to three copies to replace a work that is damaged, deteriorating, lost or stolen, or if the format of the work has become obsolete. Section 108 states that a format is considered obsolete when "the machine or device necessary to render perceptible a work stored in that format is no longer manufactured, or is no longer reasonably available in the commercial marketplace."[5] However, before making the replacement copy, the library must make a reasonable effort to see if they can locate an unused replacement at a fair price. Note that the language states "unused," which means that the library does not have to scour used book stores for a replacement copy. They also have to make a reasonable effort, which again does not require them to exhaust every book catalog. The statute is specific in that the work should be obtained for a "fair price." There are no guidelines provided as what would reasonably constitute a fair price. However, libraries should look at what is customary in the industry to gather information as to what would be considered fair in the marketplace.

When works are unpublished, a library can make up to three copies but solely for preservation and security purposes or for deposit in another library or archives for research use. The original work being copied must be currently in the collection of the library or archives that is making the copy. For example, an archives that has unpublished poems by famous Irish poet Seamus Heaney may make a copy for patrons to use while keeping the originals in a preserved and secure environment.

There is an additional rule if the preservation copy that is being made is digital. For both published and unpublished works, a digital preservation copy may not be "made available to the public in that format outside the premises of the library or archives."[6] Confusion results in the interpretation of "outside the premises." There are universities that have multiple libraries and restrict the online access to patrons in those libraries, whereas other institutions read the language a bit more strictly and do not allow access outside the physical library building where the original material is located. This restriction is a bone of contention in the library world and generates very heated debates.

There is one other part of the libraries exception that is commonly referred to as "the copy machines in the library" section. Libraries will not be held liable for copyright infringement of uses made of unsupervised reproducing equipment provided there is a notice on the equipment that alerts the user that copies made may be subject to U.S. copyright law. The statute specifically states "reproducing equipment," which is much broader than just copy machines. Any public unsupervised equipment that is capable of making reproductions in addition to copy machines, such as scanners, printers, and so on, should display such a notice. A common example of the language in the notice is "Notice: The Copyright Law of the United States (Title 17, U.S. Code) governs the making of photocopies or other reproductions of copyrighted materials. The person using this equipment is liable for any infringement." A concern among library staff is whether or not they have an affirmative duty to intervene should they observe a patron copying an entire work or something else that they consider to be infringing. The key to this provision in section 108 is that the equipment is *unsupervised*. If staff are monitoring what is being reproduced, then this clause would not be applicable. Another aspect of this is that the staff do not know what is being reproduced or why. The patron could be making a legal copy. It is the patron's responsibility to make that determination not library staff.

Librarians have struggled with interpreting and applying some of the provisions of section 108 to digital works. Of particular angst is the preservation restriction of not allowing a digital replacement copy to be viewed outside the physical space of the library. In 2005 the register of the U.S. Copyright

Office convened a group to determine what changes should be made to section 108. The group, known as the Section 108 study group, conducted extensive studies including holding public meetings in Washington, D.C., and California to understand the concerns of those affected by section 108. In 2008 the group submitted their report to the Librarian of Congress but as of yet no action has been taken on those recommendations. There is justifiable concern in the library community that opening this section up for discussion and revision could prove more harmful than helpful, especially under the current Congress.[7]

## FAIR USE, SECTION 107

Another critically important exception in the U.S. Copyright Act to libraries and others in higher education is fair use. This section of the law is applicable to a wide range of issues raised in universities. The provision will be discussed in detail here as well as in other chapters.

Fair use is an exception that can be applied in a variety of situations. Those in education, corporations, and small businesses, as well as individuals, make fair-use determinations on a regular basis and at times probably do not even realize that they are doing so. The use of copyrighted works is part of most people's daily lives, whether it is by participating on social media sites or making copies of protected works for students in a classroom. Libraries face fair-use dilemmas every day, so it is crucial that all staff have a working knowledge of the concept.

Section 107 of the U.S. Copyright Act is the fair use exception. It states:

> Notwithstanding the provisions of sections 106 and 106A, the fair use of a copyrighted work, including such use by reproduction in copies or phonorecords or by any other means specified by that section, for purposes such as criticism, comment, news reporting, teaching (including multiple copies for classroom use), scholarship, or research, is not an infringement of copyright. In determining whether the use made of a work in any particular case is a fair use the factors to be considered shall include—
>
> (1) the purpose and character of the use, including whether such use is of a commercial nature or is for nonprofit educational purposes;
> (2) the nature of the copyrighted work;
> (3) the amount and substantiality of the portion used in relation to the copyrighted work as a whole; and
> (4) the effect of the use upon the potential market for or value of the copyrighted work.

The fact that a work is unpublished shall not itself bar a finding of fair use if such finding is made upon consideration of all the above factors.

Fair use was not part of copyright law until the 1976 Act. Until then, the doctrine of fair use was determined by case law. The first fair use case was *Folsom v. Marsh* in 1841.[8] Justice Story identified the fair-use concept and set the stage for identifying the current factors that are taken into account in a fair-use analysis.

Fair use is about applying specific factors identified in both statutory and case law to the use of a work. If the use is fair, then one does not need to seek permission or pay royalties to the copyright holder. There are four factors that one must take into consideration when applying fair use. Each factor is looked at separately and weighs either in favor of fair use or against. After looking at all four factors add them up and if the majority of the factors weigh in favor of fair use, then one should be able to go ahead and use the work without asking permission. If there is only one factor that weighs in favor of fair use, then it is probably in the best interest of the user to seek permission from the copyright holder. A dilemma usually arises when there are two factors in favor and two factors against. This is the time that one must take stock of how risk averse one is and how much liability one wants to assume. Many times users do not want to incur any risk whatsoever, so they will automatically seek permission for their use of the copyrighted work.

The application of the factors is not quite as easy and straightforward as one would think. The first factor looks at the *purpose and character* of the use. Is the use for a nonprofit educational purpose or a commercial one? The first factor will weigh in favor of fair use if it is for nonprofit educational use. Commercial uses of a copyrighted work may still be fair use when weighing all four factors, but generally does not win on this first factor. Another aspect of the first factor is what is referred to as transformative use. If the work is being transformed or made into something new, then courts have favored this type of use under the first factor. Keep in mind that the purpose of copyright is to encourage people to create new works and more often than not those new works are based upon earlier works or the creative endeavors of others. Parodies, which are humorous imitations of an original work, are considered transformative works. Not all parodies or transformative works are automatically considered fair use. However, the U.S. Supreme Court recognized the importance of transformative use in the landmark 1994 decision of *Campbell v. Acuff-Rose Music, Inc.*[9] The band 2 Live Crew made a parody of Roy Orbison's famous song "Oh, Pretty Woman." When they were sued for copyright infringement they offered fair use as their defense. The Court looked closely at all four factors but weighed heavily in favor of the first factor. Even though the use was of a commercial nature, the work was quite transformative.

The second factor looks to the *nature* of the work. Is the work more factual than creative? If so, then since copyright does not protect facts, the use would weigh in favor of fair use. The more creative a work is the more protection it receives under this factor. Another aspect to the nature factor is whether or not the work is published or unpublished. The copyright holder makes the determination as to when their work is first published or made available to the public. Once it is published, then the courts will tend to view the use as fair as part of the analysis of this factor. Courts will look more closely at the use of an unpublished work and provide it with more protection. This was evident in the 1987 case of *Salinger v. Random House*,[10] where a biographer wanted to paraphrase excerpts from letters that were penned by noted author J. D. Salinger. The recipients of the letters had donated them to various university library departments of special collections, which is how the biographer obtained access to them. The Court found that the unpublished nature of the work weighed quite heavily in their decision to decide against fair use in the case. There was great concern that the Salinger ruling would mean that no unpublished works would ever be subject to fair use. So, in 1992, Congress amended section 107 to including the following statement: "The fact that a work is unpublished shall not itself bar a finding of fair use if such finding is made upon consideration of all . . . factors."[11] This amendment allows courts to consider the unpublished nature of a work, but being unpublished does not automatically bar a finding of fair use.

The *amount and substantiality* of the portion used of the copyrighted work is the third factor. The law does not provide magic numbers of word counts, pages, or percentages. One must decide how much is needed to accomplish their purpose. At times using an entire work could be fair use. The Court in the *American Geophysical Union v. Texaco* case ruled that a journal article was an entire work.[12] Using a photograph or image would be an entire work and thus might not qualify for fair use under this factor. However, courts have ruled that a thumbnail size or images that have low resolution may qualify for fair use. The Ninth Circuit case of *Kelly v. Arriba Soft Corporation* addressed this specific issue.[13] Kelly, a commercial photographer sold his images through his website. A search engine indexed Kelly's pictures and returned thumbnail-size images of them when users browsed the web for images. When the user would click on the image it would take them to Kelly's website where they could see the images in the full size. The Court ruled that such use would be a fair use. Another twist when trying to determine how much use of a work would be fair use is the concept of the "heart of the work." There are times when a very small amount has great significance and using that amount would not be fair use. There was a famous Supreme Court case[14] involving former president Gerald Ford. He had written a memoir, *A Time to Heal*, which was to be published by Harper & Row. Before the work was published, The *Nation* magazine obtained a copy of Ford's manuscript and published a news article quoting approximately three hundred words from the five-hundred page book. Even though that was an extremely insignificant amount number wise, the passage that was used was extremely significant to the work as a whole. The passage used was the reasoning behind President Ford's pardon of President Nixon. The Court believed that this was one of the most important parts of Ford's book and constituted the heart of the work.

The final fair-use factor is *market effect*. What effect does the copy that is being made have on the market for the original work? Would it be considered a substitution for the original work? Is the copy harming the market for the original work? These are all questions that must be asked when applying the fourth fair-use factor. Trying to assess the market can be challenging at times. Using a small portion of a work for educational purposes might not impact the market, but copying chapters of books or journal articles could, particularly if there are licensing mechanisms in place to provide the copyright holder with royalties.

All four of the above factors must be applied to each use of a copyrighted work. There are situations where the application of fair use is easy but most times it is complex. Situations that occur in libraries will sometimes use the libraries exception or may use fair use or even a combination of both to achieve the final result. Issues that libraries frequently encounter are discussed below with a copyright analysis and some suggested options.

## LIBRARY ISSUES

### E-Reserves

Placing items on reserve is certainly not a novel idea. It is a long-standing tradition in libraries for professors to put required and supplementary readings on reserve for students to access. Generally, these readings were in addition to a required textbook for the course that the students would purchase. It could include library books, professor's personal copies of books, book chapters, issues of journals, journal articles, class lecture notes, student papers, case studies, and so on. Of course, the materials were in print and libraries for the most part had figured out how to handle the copyright issues. Now, there are electronic reserves and libraries struggle with what they see as new rules in copyright. The copyright law has not changed but the analysis and application of it has, given that there is an increased use of technology.

In the mid-1990s when libraries started offering e-reserves options, publishers became quite wary of this, concerned that there would be a decline in their revenue. They initially tried to draft guidelines for e-reserves as part of the Conference on Fair Use in 1994, but none of the parties could agree on the terms, so the guidelines were never adopted. Publishers via the Association of American Publishers (AAP) became quite aggressive in protecting their assets by issuing thinly veiled threats of legal action in the guise of complaints to targeted college and university libraries that had implemented electronic reserve systems.[15] One of the first institutions that received a complaint was the University of California, San Diego. Cornell went public with their guidelines that AAP agreed to in 2006.[16] The Cornell guidelines were actually broader than just e-reserves. They also incorporated electronic course content. Two years later in 2008, Hofstra, Marquette, and Syracuse followed Cornell's lead in drafting guidelines that satisfied AAP in an attempt to avoid litigation.

The publishers continued to pursue agreements with universities but hit a roadblock when they approached Georgia State University (GSU) about their e-reserves system. GSU had discussions with the publishers who had complained in part that the e-reserves had no password protection and that anyone could access the materials. GSU acquiesced to their recommendation and required passwords to access the e-reserves materials. The publishers were not satisfied with that and filed suit against GSU in April 2008 in the U.S. District Court for the Northern District of Georgia in Atlanta which is in the Eleventh Circuit.[17] The specific publishers that brought suit were Cambridge University Press, Oxford University Press, and Sage Publications. They claimed that GSU had listed 6,700 items on reserve for the spring 2008 semester and although they acknowledged that some of these were print reserves, they argued that the majority were electronic and infringed on their copyright. They claimed that the infringement had been ongoing and provided examples dating from the fall 2006 semester through spring 2008. The publishers argued that the posting of digital excerpts exceeded fair use and required GSU to license for the use. GSU argued that their use of the excerpts was sanctioned by the fair-use section of the U.S. Copyright Act. It is important to note that although the case was brought on behalf of the three publishers listed above, the plaintiffs' litigation was funded 50 percent by the AAP and 50 percent by the Copyright Clearance Center (CCC),[18] both of which have a vested financial interest in the outcome.

In 2009 GSU revised its copyright policy and adopted a fair-use checklist[19] to help guide faculty in determining whether their use was fair or not under the fair-use exception to the U.S. Copyright Act. In order to have a finite group of works to assess, the judge in the case required the parties to compile a list of the publishers' works that had been posted on the e-reserves site for the two semesters following the adoption of the new policy. Only books were to be analyzed and not journal articles. There were initially ninety-nine excerpts that had been identified, but the plaintiffs chose to submit only seventy-five of those ninety-nine for the judge's review. The trial began in May 2011, and Judge Evans handed down her 350-page decision in May 2012.

In order to succeed in a claim of infringement, the publishers had to prove that they had a valid copyright in the books, whether directly, through a license, or an assignment of copyright from the author. There were books where they could not prove that they had a valid copyright, so there could be no infringement if there was no ownership of copyright. After determining if there was a valid copyright Judge Evans applied the fair-use analysis to each use of the work. Prior to analyzing each work, she provided an overall fair-use analysis and description of how she would decide if there was an infringement.

For the first factor of purpose and character the publishers argued that making a mirror image copy is not transformative so should not win under this factor. They cited the Supreme Court in *Campbell v. Acuff Rose*, which ruled that a transformative work such as the parody before them was fair use. The publishers also cited the Kinko's,[20] Michigan Document Service (MDS),[21] and Texaco[22] cases as directly on point to support their argument that fair use does not apply on this factor. The Kinko's and Michigan Document Service decisions are well-known course pack cases. Kinko's, a commercial copy shop, was sued by Basic Books in 1991 for photocopying book chapters that were included in course packs. The course packs were a compilation of book chapters, articles, and so on. The readings were selected by professors and provided to Kinko's to copy. Students would purchase them for the course directly from Kinko's. The court ruled against Kinko's on three of the four fair-use factors. The court ruled that the purpose was for commercial use: the amount ranging from 5 to 25 percent of a work was excessive; and the market was harmed since students would not purchase the original work. They ruled in favor of Kinko's only on the second factor, which is the nature of the work. The works were for courses like history and sociology, which are more factual in nature. The MDS case was similar to Kinko's in that it was a commercial copy shop but more of a mom-and-pop business operating out of Ann Arbor, Michigan, and producing course packs for the University of Michigan. They too lost the fair-use argument but on all four factors, not just the three in Kinko's. The Texaco case discussed earlier was not a course pack case but a situation where a scientist employed by Texaco made copies of journal articles that had been circulated by the company for his research.

The court in *Texaco* ruled that three factors weighed against fair use and only one in favor of fair use. The purpose, even though educational, was ultimately for commercial purposes: each article constituted an entire work, so the amount exceeded what would be considered fair; and there was an impact on the market given that there were licenses available to purchase copies of the works. The only factor in favor of fair use was the nature of the works, since the works were considered factual. The court in GSU ruled, contrary to the publisher's interpretation of *Campbell*, that the Court also stated in that case that multiple copies is the obvious statutory exception under fair use to transformative uses. Judge Evans also ruled that making multiple copies for classroom use and supporting research at a nonprofit educational institution was the purpose of the first fair-use factor. Factor one favors GSU.

For the second factor of nature the publishers argued that fair use does not apply to scholarly works, since they are so creative in nature. The court looked at both the Kinko's case and the MDS case. The court in Kinko's ruled that scholarly works were more factual in nature and thus weighed in favor of fair use. However, the court in MDS ruled the opposite way in that scholarly works are creative. The Kinko's decision was from the Southern District of New York, which is in the Second Circuit and the MDS case was from the Sixth Circuit in Michigan, neither of which hold precedence in the Eleventh Circuit, where the GSU case was being tried. It is the judge's decision as to which, if any, case to rule in a similar way to, since neither were from her jurisdiction. After reviewing both cases, Judge Evans was persuaded by the logic in the Kinko's case and ruled that the GSU scholarly readings were more factual in nature. Factor two favors GSU.

The third factor of amount was rigorously debated and proved to be potentially the most difficult for libraries. The publishers had many creative arguments as to what is counted and how it is counted for this factor. They tried to persuade the court that the only pages that should be counted for a book should be just what was included in the chapters. It should not include the index, title page, and such. They also wanted the court to rule that chapters in edited books constituted the whole work. This is similar to the argument in the Texaco case where the court ruled that an individual article was a complete work. The publishers were attempting to parse out each work so that they could say that a higher percentage of the work was used, which might then be an infringement. The publishers also argued that the copying done by GSU far exceeded the amounts permitted by the Classroom Guidelines.[23] The Guidelines were drafted in 1976 but are not a part of the copyright law. It is an agreement among private parties as to what would be acceptable fair use. They have been widely cited and used over the intervening years but have always generated some controversy. The Classroom Guidelines will be discussed in more detail in later chapters. The court ruled that all pages are counted in books regardless of whether it is the table of contents, index, or such. Likewise, chapters in edited books are part of the whole work and would not be considered individual works. Judge Evans rejected quite quickly the Classroom Guidelines limitations saying that they were not reasonable and did not support student learning. Since the works were not transformative, she did rule that the excerpts from the works used must be decidedly small and must not be the heart of the work in order to be fair use. In this case Judge Evans defined decidedly small as only using one chapter of a book if it is ten or more chapters and 10 percent of the book if it has less than ten chapters. The publishers also argued that repeated use of the same work semester after semester should weigh against fair use. Judge Evans dismissed that rationale saying that it would be "an impractical, unnecessary limitation." She understood that some works are classics and would be used every semester that the course was offered. GSU would win on this factor if the amount fell within the guidelines articulated by the court.

In the final fair-use factor of market effect the publishers argued that the Copyright Clearance Center (CCC) provided reasonable access to the materials. They also claimed that they suffered such great financial harm that they would have to go out of business. The court weighed four different questions regarding market harm. Did the use of the excerpted works adversely affect the potential *market* for the copyrighted work? Did the use adversely affect the potential *value* of the copyrighted work? Does the copy substitute for the original? Is the harm to the potential market significant? The court's analysis of this factor decided that the larger the excerpt, the greater the potential harm to the market. Since she had instituted the 10 percent or one chapter guideline, that would not be a substitute for the original work. Judge Evans understood that licenses can be available for excerpts of works, but her criteria included that the works available under a license agreement must be easily accessible, reasonably priced, and in the format that is reasonably convenient for users. The publishers had argued that the CCC or their own inventory provided such licenses. However, in the course of the trial it was shown that licenses for the book excerpts were not available from CCC during 2009. It also showed that Cambridge and Oxford combined had only thirteen digital excerpts available out of forty-six. The judge reasoned that if permissions for digital excerpts were unavailable, then there could be no harm to the market, provided of course that the digitized version by the university had restricted access to the works. Even if digital permissions were available, the unpaid use caused extremely small damage to the publisher's copyright. The standard for market harm is that there is substantial harm, so theoretically GSU should have won on this factor. However, Judge Evans imposed two additional considerations. The first was that if every university library is digitizing works for e-reserves, then there is potential substantial harm if the conduct is so widespread. It is not only GSU's actions that must be taken into consideration but what the harm is to the market if everyone is doing it. Part of GSU's defense was that this is acceptable community practice. Judge Evans was not persuaded by that argument, and in fact, it appears that it played a part in her additional considerations of market effect. Second, she raised the legal concept of equitable doctrine, which means that publishers have rights to collect fees for their works. With the additional parameters imposed, this fair-use factor would be in GSU's favor if digital permissions are unavailable and would weigh in favor of the publisher if the permissions for digital excerpts are readily available.

Some additional arguments that the publishers made were that authors would not have an incentive to publish if they were not receiving royalties. The publishers continued their argument in stating that they would not be able to publish scholarly works because they were losing so much revenue. They might even have to go out of business. Judge Evans did not buy that argument, believing that allowing unpaid, nonprofit academic use of small excerpts in controlled circumstances would not diminish the creation of academic works. She called the publishers' argument that they would be forced out of business due to the decline in permissions revenue "glib." She noted that in the financials the publishers had to supply the court only .0024 percent of their profits came from permissions revenue.

Once the general fair-use analysis had been conducted, Judge Evans then applied it to each allegedly infringing work. Out of the seventy-five works that she applied her analysis to, she ruled that only five works used by GSU infringed the publishers' copyrights. If the publishers could not prove that they had a valid copyright to the work, then it was not included in her consideration. Also, GSU had provided statistics as to how many times the work was accessed by students. If no one read the excerpt, then she reasoned that there could be no infringement. The five infringements broke down as follows:

Four chapters, which was 8.38 percent of the entire work.
Two chapters, which was 3.01 percent of the entire work.
Seven chapters, which was 12.29 percent of the entire work.
Two chapters, which was 12.5 percent of the entire work.
Two chapters, which was 8.28 percent of the entire work.

Judge Evans in announcing her ruling also looked at the purpose of copyright and articulated that free excerpts to students would further the spread of knowledge, which is the goal of copyright. In a surprising twist, she ordered the publishers to pay the court costs and attorneys fees for GSU. Usually, it is the party that loses that can be ordered to pay the costs of the litigation. This was another indicator from the court that even though GSU was found to have infringed on five works, there were seventy-one works that the publishers lost on their copyright infringement claim. The publishers have appealed the decision and that appeal is pending.

So what does the GSU decision mean for e-reserves operations in libraries? If your library is in the Eleventh Circuit, which includes Georgia, Alabama, and Florida, then the GSU decision holds great weight. However, if your library is not in the Eleventh Circuit, then the GSU decision is not legally applicable. This was a case of first impression in the Eleventh Circuit, which means that they had never adjudicated a case with the same legal questions and facts. There are no other cases in any other circuit that have ruled on the exact same legal question and set of facts, so should another circuit be confronted with the same issue, they will look to see what other circuits have decided. If this is the case, then GSU decision could have a broader reach than just the Eleventh Circuit. Also, it must be kept in mind that the GSU case only evaluated fair use for books. It did not include journal articles or other copyrighted works that are typically used in a reserves system. A legal analysis for those types of e-reserves materials has yet to be addressed by the courts.

It is important to note that Judge Evans stated that she does not like bright-line rules, which in essence set a standard for what is acceptable. So even though she specified amounts that would be acceptable in the GSU case, it does not necessarily mean that the amount is the maximum that could be used. The pedagogical purpose is critical, as is the availability of licensed works in the needed format.

To do a copyright analysis of an e-reserves issue, the following questions should be asked.

1. Does the institution have a copyright policy? If so, then this is the place to begin. If it is not a current policy that accurately reflects university activities, then it should be revised. GSU had an older policy that was quite controversial. They had the opportunity to update it during the litigation and it was the new policy that the court then reviewed.
2. Does the library have an e-reserves policy? If they do, then look closely at what it says for the process and procedures. If the policy has not been reviewed and/or updated in awhile, then this might be the time to do that. Does the policy allow for fair use to be applied each and every time, or is it only considered fair use the first time an item is placed on reserve? Does the policy dictate that all e-reserve items require permission and that the library will not rely upon fair use?

3. If the library determines that permission must be obtained before an item can be put on e-reserve, then is there a defined permission process? Who obtains permission—the library or the professor? The Copyright Clearance Center (CCC) has been designated by many publishers as their permissions agent. However, the CCC does not represent all publishers and sometime not even all the works from publishers they have agreements with. How are the permissions retained and for how long? Are the permissions for onetime use or for multiple-semester use?

4. Is the policy being consistently implemented across the campus or campuses? It is critical that all employees understand and follow the policy. When the AAP approached the various universities about their e-reserves services, one of the issues that universities ran into is that they were not consistently following their own policy across campuses.

5. Do faculty complete forms to put an item on e-reserves? Do they use the fair-use checklist that is now currently utilized by GSU and other universities? If so, does any library employee check the veracity of the completed forms? How long are the forms retained? Who retains them? Many institutions have record retention policies, so libraries should check to see if their institution has one and if so whether such records fall under the provisions of such a policy.

6. Is there restricted access to the e-reserves, or can anyone access them? If it can be restricted to just the students enrolled in the class, it is better for a fair-use argument in terms of the market-effect factor.

7. Is the e-reserves item protected by copyright? If the work is a U.S. federal government work, then there is no copyright and it can be used on e-reserves without a problem. Likewise, if the work was published in the United States prior to 1923, then it is in the public domain. A question that can sometimes arise in this context is if the original work is public domain but was scanned by a third party, is it still public domain or does the party that scanned the document have any rights to it? Generally, once the work is public domain, then it remains so regardless of someone scanning it.

8. If the work is protected by copyright, then the library must start looking at the available options. Can e-reserves link to an item instead of having the actual copy in the system? Linking is always preferable.

9. Is the item in digital form part of a library subscription? If so, check the license for the database that contains the item to see if e-reserves is expressly allowed or prohibited.

10. If the digital item is not part of the library subscription, then where and how was the item obtained? Was the item purchased by the library,

the professor, or someone else? Are there any restrictions on the use of such an item?

11. If the item is in paper format, is there a digital copy available? If not, then who scans the item? How long does the library retain a copy of the scanned item?

12. How much of a work will the library put on reserve? An article is considered an entire work, but most times the entire article is what is needed. However, with books, the GSU court suggested that one chapter out of a book that contains ten or more chapters and 10 percent of a book that has less than ten chapters is fair use. Is that the maximum amount of a book that will be allowed on e-reserves, or will decisions be on a case-by-case basis?

13. Will e-reserves be limited to text formats or will audiovisual, music, and images be allowed? How do you define acceptable amounts in those formats?

E-reserves can be a minefield if there is not a well-thought-out and coordinated effort to address the issues before instituting an e-reserves program or to reevaluate one that is already in existence.

### Conversion of VHS Tapes to DVDs

Formats that encapsulate copyrighted content seem to change from year to year. An issue that is raised repeatedly is whether or not it is legal to convert VHS tapes to DVDs. There are plenty of reasons given as to why they must be converted. For example,

1. DVDs are a preferable format.
2. VHS machines are considered outdated and we are not allowed to purchase VHS equipment.
3. The classrooms no longer support VHS equipment.
4. VHS players are no longer available to purchase.
5. Need to make copies just in case something should happen to the original.
6. Patrons that want to borrow the content only have DVD players.
7. The VHS tape is starting to deteriorate and it needs to be preserved.

Those are all very practical reasons for wanting to make the conversion. However, the copyright law doesn't necessarily take into consideration the argument that it's just easier to use a DVD. If a library is looking to convert a VHS to a DVD, then section 108 of the U.S. Copyright Act is generally the controlling law, provided that the library qualifies for the section 108 exception.

Here are some questions to consider when analyzing a conversion issue:

1. The first question that always must be asked is what is the reason for the conversion? If it is solely for convenience, then that is not covered under section 108.
2. Is the purpose of the conversion for preservation purposes?
3. If so, is the work considered published or unpublished?
4. If the work is published, then:
   a. Is the work currently damaged, deteriorating, lost, or stolen? If it is, then it is a potential candidate for libraries to make up to three replacement copies of it.
   b. Is the format obsolete? VHS tapes are not obsolete since VHS players can still be purchased in the marketplace. So this reason would not be a valid one under section 108.
   c. Has the library conducted a reasonable investigation to locate an unused copy at a fair price? The law does not require that the library search every avenue for a replacement copy but only a reasonable investigation. It is also specified that the copy does not have to be a used copy. If after a reasonable investigation, an unused copy is located, then is the price fair? Section 108 does not require that the library purchase a copy at what the market would consider an exorbitant price, only a fair price. Librarians can certainly ascertain what a fair price is in the current market. However, if such a copy is located then, the library cannot make a replacement copy but instead must purchase the one that is available in the marketplace.
   d. Is the conversion for preservation of a damaged VHS tape, and an unused one at a fair price cannot be located? If so, then the library can make up to three replacement copies in the same format. This means that it is converted from VHS to VHS.
   e. Does the library want to make a DVD copy? If the library meets all the criteria in (d) but wants to make a digital copy of the VHS tape, then they can do that but subject to restrictions. The digital copy cannot be made available to the public outside the physical confines of the library. Patrons may only use the digital copy in the library. It cannot be circulated outside the library. It can also not be posted on a website that is available or accessible beyond the physical library.
   f. Is the copy damaged, or is this an attempt to have an extra copy just in case something happens to the original? Making copies in anticipation of a VHS tape being damaged or destroyed does not

meet the criteria described above, so this type of activity would not
be allowed.
5. Is the work unpublished? It might sound unusual for a VHS tape to be
   unpublished, but it can happen. The unpublished piece, though, is more
   typical of personal papers, manuscripts, and such.
   a. If unpublished, does the library currently have the work in their col-
      lection? If they do, then they are allowed to make up to three copies,
      but the copies must be solely for preservation or security purposes
      or to deposit in another library that meets the criteria of section 108.

The general rule of thumb for conversion issues is to first attempt to purchase the work in the format that is needed or desired. The above questions
relate to conversions in library collections. There are other conversion issues
for faculty and staff that will be addressed in their respective chapters.

### International Interlibrary Loan

In recent years questions have been raised as to whether or not participating
in international interlibrary loans is legal. There are some that claim such
lending is beyond the scope of the interlibrary loan provisions of section 108.
A white paper published by the Association of Research Libraries concluded
that loaning materials to non-U.S. libraries is within the parameters of interlibrary loan.[24]

International interlibrary loan is governed by the International Federation
of Library Associations and Institutions' International Lending: Principles
and Guidelines for Procedure. The goal of the IFLA guidelines is to promote
access of published materials across nations. "The guidelines stipulate that
'all reasonable efforts should be made to satisfy international requests,' but
also affirm the importance of respect for copyright, indicating that 'each
supplying library should be aware of, and work within, the copyright laws
of its own country' and that 'requesting library should pay due regard to the
copyright laws of the supplying library's country.'"[25]

Interlibrary loan documentation from U.S. libraries usually has a statement that requires the borrower to comply with U.S. Copyright law. The
borrower checks the box and U.S. libraries fill the request, taking the
borrower at their word. There is a basic level of trust and good faith that
libraries are acting responsibly and legally. It must be noted that even if
the actual copy of the material is being sent to a non-U.S. library, the copy
itself is made in the United States, thus is subject to U.S. law. It is a point
of distinction when taking into account which country's law would apply
in such a situation.

The following questions should be considered when fulfilling international interlibrary loan requests.

1. Does the borrowing library submit a form that indicates it complies with copyright law?
2. Does the lending library have a form that indicates that it complies with copyright law?
3. Is the item being loaned subject to any copyright restrictions?
4. Does the lending library have a policy and procedure in place for fulfilling requests from non-U.S. libraries?
5. Are there consortial arrangements in place for international ILL requests? If so, do they conform with applicable laws?

As research and collaboration across borders becomes more frequent, international interlibrary loan is a critical piece to providing access to works held in countries around the world. Also, shrinking budgets for many libraries dictate that they rely upon international interlibrary loan agreements. As long as the parties to the loan understand and abide by the copyright laws of the respective countries, then international interlibrary loan helps to provide a robust research environment.

## First-Sale Doctrine

Section 109 of the U.S. Copyright Act is known as the first-sale doctrine. This section of the law is what allows libraries to loan materials and used bookstores to survive. Once the copyright owner authorizes their work to be released to the public, then copies of the work can be sold, borrowed, leased, gifted, and so forth. This does not mean that the purchaser or borrower of the work has any claim on the copyright. They only own the physical copy but not the copyright.

There are limitations to this doctrine for musical works or sound recordings that contain musical works. The music industry became concerned that if CDs were rented, then they could be copied and returned, thus bypassing purchasing them. Congress amended section 109 to address this concern. Such works are now only allowed to be rented, leased or loaned for nonprofit purposes by a nonprofit library or a nonprofit educational institution.

Two recent cases tested the application and limits of the first-sale doctrine. Even though both cases were quite different, the central question was the same. Were the copies lawfully made according to the U.S. Copyright Act?

The Supreme Court case of *Kirtsaeng v. John Wiley & Sons, Inc.*[26] involved a Cornell student from Thailand who had his family purchase copies of textbooks published by Wiley and ship them to him in the United States, since the cost of the books was significantly lower in Thailand. Kirtsaeng then turned around and sold the books on eBay for a profit in the neighborhood of $1.2 million. Wiley claimed that such an action was a violation of their copyright, but Kirtsaeng claimed that it was sanctioned under the first-sale doctrine.

Wiley's argument was that books manufactured outside the United States were not subject to U.S. copyright law. Kirtsaeng's defense was that the copies he purchased were lawfully made and the copies were protected by first sale. Libraries were quite worried that if the Supreme Court ruled in Wiley's favor, then many books on their shelves that had been manufactured outside the United States and imported would be illegal copies and have to be removed. Luckily, the Court ruled in Kirtsaeng's favor that copies that were lawfully made abroad are entitled to the benefits of section 109.

Another case involving the first-sale doctrine that could potentially impact libraries is the decision in the U.S. District Court for the Southern District of New York case of *Capitol Records v. ReDigi*.[27] The question before the court was: Can a digital music file that was lawfully made and purchased be resold by its owner through ReDigi? The company, ReDigi, was in the business of reselling user's digital music files. The user would upload their digital music file from their computer to ReDigi's server. The court ruled that in doing that they then made a copy of the work, which was an unlawful reproduction. Since the copy was not lawfully made, an infringement occurred. First-sale doctrine does not apply to digital music files in the type of situation that ReDigi created. However, the court did indicate that the sale of the device that included the lawfully made and purchased digital music files could be sold.

E-books are becoming increasingly popular. The American Library Association has reported some statistics from a Pew report that state 23 percent of Americans sixteen years of age and older read e-books.[28] There has been much controversy over e-books and how the first-sale doctrine could apply to those types of works. The problem arises because e-books are not purchased like their print counterparts. Once a library purchases the print version, they can loan it, sell it, dispose of it, and so on without any interference from the copyright owner. However libraries do not purchase the e-book. They only purchase *access* to the e-book. The publisher determines how and when the e-books can be used.

The following are some questions that should be considered when entering into an e-books agreement.

1. Are the rights granted by the publisher the same as allowed in the first-sale doctrine? If not, how similar or dissimilar are they?

2. Does the publisher allow the e-book to be loaned to multiple users at the same time, or is it restricted to one user at a time?
3. Does the access to the e-book expire after a certain period of time or number of uses?
4. Can the e-book be printed or downloaded? Are there restrictions on how much can be printed or downloaded? Are there restrictions of that per user or over the total access period?
5. What are the replacement provisions if the e-book file becomes corrupted or damaged? Do the provisions include any refunds for interrupted service?
6. Does the e-book license provide for educational and possibly commercial use? Does it allow for other uses under the copyright law such as fair use and interlibrary loan?
7. In the bigger picture, what are the library's collection development policies regarding e-books since they are transitory in nature?
8. Has the library considered the retention and preservation issues associated with e-books? Can the library retain an archival copy should the e-book disappear?
9. How does the library justify the expenditures for books that can be here today and gone tomorrow?
10. Are there provisions in the e-book license for notice from the vendor if the e-book is being removed from their inventory or if they suddenly decide to cease access?
11. Are there notifications by the vendor if the content of the e-book is changed in any way? How does the library deal with verifying the integrity of the work?

As the e-book market evolves and the demand increases, libraries have a responsibility to ensure that their patrons have long-term access to the works. Libraries are entrusted with preserving the works in whatever format for future generations, so they must be diligent in crafting e-book agreements that meet this mission.

## Archives and Special Collections

Archives and special collections in libraries pose many special copyright issues. "Copyright's influence on special collections had grown exponentially because of the rapid digitization of dissemination strategies and possibilities. That influence has stimulated both the complexity of preservation and the desire to make acceptable those unique special collections."[29] As discussed earlier in the chapter, the libraries exception, section 108, as well as fair use play a critical role in the operations of archives and special collections. However, the determination of copyright ownership in such collections is the first step in the copyright analysis.

Many university archives and special collections departments rely upon donors, typically alumni and their families, to donate works such as papers and objects to them in order to populate their collection. At first blush this appears to be a very easy, straightforward transaction. However, this is not always the case. The transfer of works to a university library usually includes a deed of gift, which specifies the terms and conditions under which the transfer will occur. It outlines the responsibilities of each party and the transfer of ownership in the works.

There are many clauses in a deed of gift, but a critical one that is sometimes overlooked is the transfer of copyright from the donor to the university. In addition to the physical object or work being transferred, it is important to obtain the copyright as well. Donors are not always the copyright owners of the works they gift to a university, but hopefully they will grant as many rights as they have.

The following are some questions that should be considered when analyzing a copyright issue for deeds of gift.

1. Is the donor transferring the copyright in the works to the university?
2. Does the donor own the copyright to the works or does the donor only have possession of a physical item? If the latter is the case, then they can only assign the rights that they have. For example, a donor might be donating letters received from famous people. Even though the donor is the recipient of the letter, he or she does not own the copyright to the letter. The person who penned the letter is the copyright owner. A case that addressed the issue is *Salinger v. Random House*.[30] Such notables as Ernest Hemingway and Judge Learned Hand had received letters from the literary giant J. D. Salinger. Both Hemingway and Hand had donated items in their possession to various university libraries. Ian Hamilton, who was a well-known literary critic and biographer, approached Salinger about writing his biography. Salinger refused. Hamilton decided to pursue the project anyway and used the Salinger letters from various university collections. He originally quoted from the letters, but due to copyright concerns, he paraphrased quite a bit. Hamilton entered into an agreement with Random House to publish the work. Salinger obtained a copy of the manuscript before it was published and filed a copyright infringement claim against Random House. The Second Circuit Court of Appeals applied a fair-use analysis and ruled in favor of Salinger. Part of the court's reasoning was that even though Hamilton paraphrased the

letters, they were unpublished, and if Salinger later decided to publish them, the public could reasonably believe that they had already read the letters, thus harming the market for Salinger. So even though the university libraries had legal copies of the letters, Salinger owned the copyright and he had not entered into any agreement with the libraries.

3. Does the donor know who owns the copyright to the works being donated? If possible, it's good to try to ascertain that information so that the library can document it for future use.

4. If the donor does own the copyright to the work but refuses to assign copyright to the library, what rights is the donor willing to transfer to the library? It's important for the library to try to obtain rights to digitize the materials, loan the materials, display the materials, and allow the public to access them.

5. If the donor is the copyright owner and is unwilling to transfer the copyright of the works at the time of the donation, ask if they would be willing to transfer it upon their death.

Deeds of gift need to be specific but broad enough to allow for unknown circumstances that might arise. Many clauses in deeds of gift are subject to interpretation. This can certainly be beneficial, but more often than not, it ties the hands of archivists, who are reluctant to move forward without a clear understanding of the donor's intent. Once the donor dies, then the deed of gift cannot be altered.

## Digitization Projects

Patrons want quick access to materials and do not necessarily want to visit the physical library to obtain them, so in addition to collecting works only in digital form, libraries are also digitizing their print collections when feasible. The barriers for libraries include high costs, lack of staff, and time constraints, as well as handling the copyright issues associated with digitization.

In 2004, it appeared that Google might have the solution to libraries' digitization issues. Google announced that they were embarking on a journey to digitize library collections and called it the Google Books Library Project. Initially, Google entered into agreements with Harvard, Oxford, Stanford, the New York Public Library (NYPL), and the University of Michigan. Google would digitize the works in their collections and in exchange would provide the libraries with a digital copy that was to be retained in a dark archive. The University of Michigan was the only entity that agreed to have their entire collection digitized. The other universities and the NYPL only provided selected works, most of which were public domain. Google had the time, money, staff, and equipment to do the large-scale digitization, theoretically thereby resolving the many issues that libraries struggled with in digitizing their collections. However, the major stumbling block was copyright. Many of the works provided to Google by Michigan were still protected by copyright.

Google scanned the materials into the project database. They allowed full-text access to works that were in the public domain but only snippets of works that were still protected by copyright. Google claimed that such scanning and distribution was covered under fair use. The Authors Guild and individual authors disagreed and filed a copyright infringement lawsuit in New York against Google in 2005.

Google's fair-use argument centers on transformative use. They also claim that the market for the works is not being harmed but in fact benefiting from the exposure of works that had long since lost their marketability in the print world. The authors disagree with that analysis. They do not see the work as transformative, since it is making a mirror image copy of a work without having any new meaning created. Google also has the capability to distribute it to millions, all without any remuneration to the authors. Google argues that their project benefits society, but the authors counter that the primary benefit is to Google, since it enhances their bottom line by generating revenue with the placement of advertisements on the web pages that display a users results.

The legal wrangling has gone on for eight years but appears to be getting closer to a resolution. There have been attempted settlement agreements that have collapsed for various reasons. In 2011 Judge Chin rejected the most recent $125 million settlement agreement because it required authors to opt out of the Google project instead of allowing them to opt in. Judge Chin did not think that was either fair or reasonable. In late September 2013 Judge Chin heard each party's fair-use arguments in a summary judgment proceeding.[31] In November, Judge Chin found in favor of Google, ruling that Google's use of copyrighted works was fair use and dismissed the case. Judge Chin wrote, "In my view Google Books provides significant public benefits."[32] The Authors Guild has appealed.

There is speculation that another Second Circuit case involving mass digitization swayed Judge Chin's ruling in Google's favor. The case is *Authors Guild v. HathiTrust*.[33] In 2008, the universities of the Committee on Institutional Cooperation (CIC) and the University of California system formed a partnership to develop a repository that would preserve the materials in their collections by digitizing them and depositing them into the repository named the HathiTrust. The CIC universities that had partnered with Google for the Library Book Project would deposit the dark archive copy of the work that had been provided to them by Google. They would then digitize other important and unique materials from their collections and add them to HathiTrust. The University of Michigan and Indiana University manage the repository. The partnership has over seventy research universities and continues to grow as more and more universities seek a place to archive and preserve some of their most valuable assets. Currently there are over ten million volumes that have been digitized and deposited into the HathiTrust. The access model is similar to Google in that only public domain works are displayed in their entirety. Only snippets of works that are still protected by copyright can be accessed. One of the major differences, though, is that the full text of copyrighted works is available to those who are blind or visually impaired.

In 2011 the Authors Guild sued HathiTrust as an entity as well as specific universities—University of Michigan, University of Wisconsin, University of California, Indiana University, and Cornell University for copyright infringement. A little over a year after the suit was filed in the Second Circuit, Judge Baer decisively ruled in favor of HathiTrust. He stated in his ruling that "I cannot imagine a definition of fair use that . . . would require that I terminate this invaluable contribution to the progress of science and cultivation of the arts that at the same time effectuates the ideals espoused by the Americans with Disabilities Act (ADA)." Judge Baer did not find that the digitization is transformative but that the access and search capabilities, which allow new uses such as text mining, qualified as a transformative use. The Authors Guild claimed that HathiTrust harmed their market. However, Judge Baer ruled that there was no viable market and no plans to develop one.[34] This was a critical recognition of the actual market and a denial of the overarching claims of the Authors Guild, which seeks to tightly control any use of a copyrighted work. Judge Baer's ruling is similar to that of Judge Evans in the Georgia State case, where she ruled that there could be no market harm if digital excerpts of the books were not reasonably available.

There are certainly some notable differences between the Google case and HathiTrust. Probably the most important one is that the universities involved in the HathiTrust litigation are nonprofit educational institutions and not commercial ventures like Google. Another important difference is that HathiTrust's mission "is to contribute to the common good by collecting, organizing, preserving, communicating, and sharing the record of human knowledge."[35] Google's mission statement is "to organize the world's information and make it universally accessible and useful."[36] HathiTrust's mission is a bit more altruistic than that of Google. Since Google is a commercial venture, it can go out of business at any time or decide that digitizing works is not lucrative enough to satisfy its shareholders. However, university libraries are in the business of preserving works for future generations in formats that are accessible and searchable. The Baer court understood quite well the different goals of the parties involved. Suffice it to say that the Authors Guild was not happy with the ruling and has filed an appeal.

On June 10, 2014, the U.S. Court of Appeals for the Second Circuit in New York ruled in favor of HathiTrust in the appeal.[37] The Court affirmed the majority of Judge Baer's ruling finding that the HathiTrust database of digital copies made for full-text searching, text mining, and access for the print-disabled is fair use.[38]

The Second Circuit discussed all four fair use factors. They found that "the creation of a full-text searchable database is a quintessentially transformative use."[39] The Court went on to say that "by enabling a full-text search, the HDL adds to the original something new with a different purpose and a different character."[40] Due to the transformative use, the Court ruled in favor of HathiTrust on the first fair use factor of purpose and character.

The Court did not spend much time on the nature of the works, which is the second factor to be considered in a fair use analysis, recognizing that the database is comprised of creative as well as factual works. They did not consider this factor all that important since creative works would also be transformed. The Court stated that their "fair use analysis hinges on the other three factors."[41]

The third fair use factor is amount. The Court looked at "whether the copying used more of the copyrighted work than necessary and whether the copying was excessive."[42] The Court did not believe that the copying was excessive since the entire work would be needed for a full-text search. The Court also found that the number of copies made by HathiTrust was not excessive. Both the University of Michigan and Indiana University have copies on their servers, both to facilitate the flow of web traffic as well as for security purposes should there be a computer problem that resulted in data loss. Due to the above rationale, the Court found in favor of HathiTrust on this factor.

The fourth fair use factor looks at the effect on the market. The issue that the Court considered was whether or not the secondary use would be a substitute for the original work. The Court concluded that it would not and ruled in favor of HathiTrust for this factor.

Access to the works for the print-disabled also was subject to a fair use analysis by the Court. Fair use was found in three out of the four factors similar to the analysis for full-text searching and mining.

The Court did not affirm Judge Baer's ruling on the Libraries' right to preserve works under the libraries exception, section 108, or under fair use. They remanded that discussion back to the lower court for analysis, based upon their determination that the Authors Guild did not have standing to bring a lawsuit on behalf of individual copyright holders for the issues raised under the preservation argument in this case.

This is a huge victory for libraries and universities who make new uses of works. Of course, the Authors Guild has the option to appeal to the Supreme Court, which could shift the outcome. However, the momentum at the moment is directly in the libraries' camp.

Many libraries have both small and large digitization projects underway. One project that many libraries have in progress or are considering is a retrospective conversion, primarily of doctoral dissertations but some are including master's theses as well. The digitized copy would be added to the institution's repository. For dissertations completed before 1978 there is some question as to whether or not the work has been "published," which was a requirement for copyright protection under the 1909 Copyright Act. There were also notice and renewal requirements that had to be met for the work to be protected. When the 1976 Copyright Act went into effect on January 1, 1978, the publication requirement was dropped. In order to have protection, the work had to be original and fixed but did not require publication. However, until March of 1989 there were still notice and renewal requirements. For those libraries doing retrospective conversion, they first have to determine if the dissertation is protected by copyright. If it is in the public domain, then digitizing it and posting it would not be an issue. However, for those works still in copyright, the question has been whether to follow the Google model and just digitize without requesting permission from the copyright owner, since attempting to locate potentially thousands of alumni would be quite time consuming and might not be all that successful, or not digitize and post on websites without the explicit permission of the copyright owner. A Tenth Circuit Court of Appeals decision handed down on December 23, 2013, might provide some guidance to libraries with this conundrum.[43] A graduate student, Andrew Diversey, sued the University of New Mexico for illegally copying and distributing his dissertation without his permission. Copies were made of Diversey's dissertation without his permission and placed in the library. The library listed the dissertation in its catalog and made the work available to the public, thus constituting a distribution. The University claimed fair use, but the court disagreed with them, finding only the first factor of purpose and character in their favor. There were certainly other elements to this case, but the court's message was quite clear that it is only the author who can authorize copies to be made. If the author does not give permission and copies are subsequently made, then they are illegal copies and any distribution of the illegal copies would be an infringement. Libraries should consider the court's rational in the Diversey case in their analysis when weighing the pros and cons of moving forward with digitizing dissertations.

In 2011, the U.S. Copyright Office issued a report on mass digitization projects and the legal issues associated with them.[44] The document was released prior to the rulings in the Georgia State and HathiTrust cases. However, it is a good snapshot of what projects are underway both nationally and internationally. It also provides the rationale for moving forward with such projects.

If your library is considering a digitization project, the following are some questions that should be considered.

1. What is the purpose of the digitization? Is it for convenience or is there a valid reason?
2. What is the scope of the digitization? Is it a collection in a certain discipline or the entire library collection?
3. What types of materials are under consideration for digitization? Is it books, journal articles, music, video, gray literature? Digitizing non-print materials raises other issues under the U.S. Copyright Act.
4. How much of the work will be digitized? Is it the entire work or only a portion of it?
5. Are the works still protected by copyright, or are they in the public domain? If they are public domain works, then they are not protected by copyright and the library does not need permission to digitize.
6. If the works are protected by copyright, who owns the copyright? Is it your institution? For example, it could be works published by your university press or an in-house publication. It might be materials in special collections where the donor has transferred copyright to the university. If the university owns the copyright, then there should be no barriers to digitization.
7. If the works are not public domain and the copyright is not owned by the institution, then what exception(s) under the Copyright Act will the university rely on to digitize the materials?
8. Are the works being digitized because they are damaged and need to be preserved? If it's a preservation issue, then section 108 could be used to justify the digitization. However, keep in mind that if section 108 is relied upon in this situation, then the digital copy is not allowed to be used beyond the physical confines of the library.
9. Will the digitized works serve another purpose, such as those in the HathiTrust or for e-reserves? Fair use would be the legal exception that could potentially apply and allow for the digitization.
10. What kind of liability is the institution willing to assume? Many universities are risk averse and will not rely on the exceptions in the Copyright Act. Instead they might require that any digitization projects obtain permission from the copyright holder before proceeding.

11. What is the capability of the library to do the scanning/digitizing in-house? The cost of equipment and staff time needed to do the work can be quite high. If the project is outsourced, what are the terms of the contract with the vendor? Will the vendor digitize works when the library does not own the copyright? Does the vendor retain a copy of the digitized work? If so, what are the parameters around their use of the work and any other rights they might demand? Will the materials be destroyed when they are scanned? What provisions are there in the contract if damage occurs or if the scans are defective? Are they requiring the university to assume all legal responsibility should they be sued for copyright infringement or any other legal challenges?

There are many copyright issues associated with digitization projects both small and large. It is important to understand what those issues are and what legal theory one will use to justify the digitization. It is also in the best interest of the institution to do a risk analysis to determine how much risk they are willing to assume. The question becomes does the benefit outweigh the risk?

## Institutional Repositories/Open Access

Universities want to document and measure the intellectual output of primarily their faculty but also students and professional staff. To this end institutional repositories, which are generally organized and managed by libraries, have been developed on campuses to capture this output. Sometimes the repositories can be subject/discipline based and other times they are comprehensive. Initially many institutions populated their repositories with what was considered gray literature, such as technical reports or bulletins from various academic units. However, as open-access initiatives grew in strength, universities began to view their repositories in a different light.

Open access means allowing scholarly works to be freely available and accessible to the world. The focus has mainly been on peer-reviewed scholarly journal articles but in recent years has broadened to include all types of scholarly works. The open-access movement received a major boost in 2008 when Harvard's Faculty of Arts and Sciences voted to provide a nonexclusive license to Harvard to make copies of their articles publicly available. Also in 2008 the National Institutes of Health (NIH) adopted their public-access policy. This policy mandated that all final peer-reviewed manuscripts that were a result of NIH funding must be made publicly available by depositing them into the National Library of Medicine's PubMed Central within twelve months of publication. Between the NIH mandate and Harvard's commitment to open access, many other universities took notice and began crafting their own open-access policies.

Other agencies within the federal government began to assess their open-access options. The rationale behind having the major federal agencies provide open access is that since the public pays for the research they should be able to benefit from the result of that research without having to pay again for it. Since 2008 there were some legislative attempts to require agencies to follow NIH's lead, but they never reached fruition. However, in 2013, the White House's Office of Technology and Information Policy (OTIP) issued a directive to all federal agencies that have in excess of $100 million in research and development to draft open-access policies.[45] The drafts were due to OTIP in the late summer of 2013 and should be released for public review sometime in 2014. There is a parallel legislative initiative working its way through Congress. The bill, The Fair Access to Science and Technology Act, known as FASTR, is similar to the White House directive.[46] The bill is still in committee. Strategically, having a law instead of relying solely on the White House directive would potentially be a stronger statement and longer-term commitment to open access, since the next president could easily rescind the directive. It would not be quite so easy to change a law.

Librarians have been major proponents of the open-access movement and have lobbied not only the U.S. government but private publishers, disciplinary societies, and university presses to jump on the open-access band wagon. There has been some limited success, but the government initiatives should assist with this initiative.

University institutional repositories are the logical place to deposit open-access works by their faculty, students, and staff or at the very minimum provide a complete citation, metadata, and link to an external repository such as PubMed Central for the full-text access to the work. However, as the federal agencies begin to release their open-access policies, central repository options are being considered. The Association of American Publishers (AAP) has begun to develop a repository called "CHORUS," which would collect all of the open-access works produced as a result of federal agencies' open-access mandates. The publishers envision this as a one-stop-shopping option. However, there is great concern from the library community that publishers would have such control and eventually find a way to somehow hold hostage the supposedly publicly available federally funded research. The Association of Research Libraries in collaboration with the Association of American Universities and the Association of Public and Land-Grant Universities are offering a different model from CHORUS called the Shared Access Research Ecosystem (SHARE).[47] This is a model of a cross-institutional repository.

Copyright and licensing are major issues in institutional repository and open-access initiatives. Institutional repositories (IRs) by their very nature are open access. One of the purposes of them is to allow the works to be freely accessible to anyone in the world. However, IRs must have the appropriate rights in order to allow that access. If the university owns the copyright to the work or the faculty has assigned them a license, which is a requirement of many university open-access policies, then there is no issue. However, many times the owner of the copyright is not the depositor. A typical scenario is when a faculty member wants to deposit his or her work in the IR but has transferred the copyright to a publisher. In such a case, universities generally require that the depositor sign a nonexclusive license granting the university the right to display and preserve the work as well as acknowledge that they have the authority to deposit the work.

If the library plans on developing an institutional repository, the following questions should be considered:

1. What is the scope of the repository? Will it house works from only those who are associated with the university or will it be broader? Is there a time limit on works that will be collected? For example, will it be only the most recent five years of a depositor's publications or everything they have produced during their career at that institution?
2. What types of works will be accepted for the repository? Will it be restricted to scholarly peer-reviewed journal articles or anything that the depositor has written?
3. Will the depositors be required to supply proof that they have the authority to deposit the work in the IR? For example, many depositors have transferred their copyright to publishers, so how will that be handled? If the depositor can locate the contract that transferred the rights to the publisher, who on the IR staff will determine if there is language in the contract that allows the depositor to make the deposit? If the depositor cannot locate the contract, then how will the IR staff handle that situation?
4. Is there a formal written agreement between the IR and the depositor that details the rights the depositor is giving to the IR? If so, who crafted the language? Is it someone who has the authority and legal background to draft the document?
5. What rights does the IR need from the depositor? Generally the depositor will grant a nonexclusive perpetual royalty-free license to the university to display and preserve the work in any format now known or later developed. There is also usually a statement that asserts that the depositor has acknowledged and identified and has permission to

include any third-party content included in the work as well as the authority to deposit the work. Since it is a nonexclusive license, it is usually acknowledged that such agreement does not transfer copyright in the work to the university.

Institutional repositories provide a great resource to a university. However, it is incumbent upon the libraries to understand and address the complex rights issues that abound in such an initiative.

## E-Resource Licensing

The era of libraries collecting primarily print materials is slowly disappearing. Electronic resources are the materials of choice in today's libraries. This shift in collection development poses many challenges as to ownership and access to a library's collection. Once a library purchased a book, a journal, a video, or a CD, they could retain that work for as long as they wanted. Under section 109 of the U.S. Copyright Act,[48] they could loan that material to as many patrons that wanted to borrow it. However, electronic resources are not owned by the library. Access to the resources and use of the resources are governed by licenses.

Many licenses for electronic resources are quite complex and lengthy. Licenses are legal documents and the terms used are sometimes foreign to the library employee who has been charged with negotiating and managing the libraries licenses. The vendors draft the licenses for their products and in doing so ensure that the terms of the license provide the most benefits to them and not the library. There is standard language in licenses, such as the term of the license, which laws and courts the library will have to abide by should there be a material breach of the license, and how and when the license can be terminated.[49] There are various phrases regarding copyright that are generally inserted into the license and which the library employee should be aware of and understand. Some resources are governed by what is commonly referred to as "shrink wrapped" or "click-through" licenses. Generally there is no paper license that is negotiated. If the purchaser breaks the wrapping on the item, be it a CD, DVD, or computer software program, or clicks "I Agree" for a web-based license, then the purchaser is bound by the terms of those agreements.

A question at the center of licensing discussions is what role copyright plays in licenses. Does a license trump copyright? When negotiating or entering into a license for library databases consider the following questions on copyright:

1. Is there any language in the license on copyright other than a statement of copyright ownership of the vendor's product?

2. If there is no copyright language, then what uses might need to be made of the product? Are any copyright issues associated with them?
3. Does the library staff member signing the license have the signatory authority to do so? Some universities place a dollar limit on what can be agreed to by certain levels of staff. Once it exceeds that limit then the library administration and/or university administration must sign and approve it.
4. Is there a global statement in the license similar to "The user will abide by the U.S. Copyright Act"? This is the type of statement that allows the most flexibility for the library.
5. Are there very specific statements such as "The user will abide by section 108 (libraries exception) of the U.S. Copyright Act" or "the user will abide by section 107 (fair use) of the U.S. Copyright Act"? Be wary of licenses that have specific sections of the copyright law included in the agreement. This could potentially restrict the libraries use to only that part of the copyright law.
6. Does the license prohibit interlibrary loan of the materials? If so, then a library should be cautious in agreeing to this if they do not have the capability to monitor the activities. Library staff might not be aware of the restrictions and fill requests, which would be a breach of the license subject to whatever penalties are agreed to by both parties.
7. Does the license require the library to guarantee or warrant that all users will comply with the copyright law? This would be an impossible clause to implement.

Licenses can trump copyright if this is specifically addressed. If the license is silent on a specific use of the materials, then there is the possibility that such use would be within the license terms as allowed under U.S. copyright law. Negotiating licenses is not for the faint of heart, but it pays to be persistent. It is not wise to agree to terms that the library cannot adhere to.

## CONCLUSION

The situations described above are common ones that librarians grapple with on any given day. There are certainly new ones that crop up, but a basic understanding of the copyright law and the general questions that should be asked will assist in defining an approach. It's also quite beneficial to have the necessary discussions with all the parties involved before embarking on a major initiative involving copyright.

## NOTES

1. U.S. Copyright Act, 17. U.S.C. § 108.
2. U.S. Copyright Act, 17. U.S.C. § 108 (a) (3).
3. U.S. National Commission on New Technological Uses of Copyrighted Works, *Final Report* (Washington, DC: Library of Congress, 1979).
4. U.S. Copyright Act, 17. U.S.C. § 108 (i).
5. U.S. Copyright Act, 17. U.S.C. § 108 (d).
6. U.S. Copyright Act, 17. U.S.C. § 108 (b)(2).
7. M. A. Brown, "Copyright Exceptions for Libraries in the Digital Age: U.S. Copyright Office Considers Reform of Section 108, Highlights of the Symposium," *College and Research Libraries News* 74 no. 4 (2013): 199–214, accessed April 10, 2014, http://crln.acrl.org/content/74/4/199.full.
8. Folsom v. Marsh, 9 F.Cas. 342 (C.C.D. Mass. 1841).
9. Campbell v. Acuff-Rose Music, Inc., 510 U.S. 569 (1994).
10. Salinger v. Random House, Inc. 811 F.2d 90 (2d Cir. 1987)
11. U.S. Copyright Act, 17 U.S.C. §107.
12. American Geophysical Union v. Texaco, Inc., 60 F.3d 913 (2d Cir. 1994), cert. dismissed, 516 U.S. 1005 (1995).
13. Kelly v. Arriba Soft Corporation, 336 F.3d 811 (9th Cir. 2003).
14. Harper & Row Publishers, Inc. v. Nation Enterprises, 471 U.S. 539 (1985).
15. A. R. Albanese, "A Failure to Communicate," *Publishers Weekly*, June 14, 2010, accessed April 10, 2014, http://www.publishersweekly.com/pw/by-topic/industry-news/publisher-news/article/43500-a-failure-to-communicate.html.
16. L. Rice, "C.U. Changes E-Reserve Policy to Avoid Lawsuit," *Cornell Daily Sun*, October 3, 2006, accessed April 10, 2014, http://cornellsun.com/node/18733.
17. Cambridge University Press et al. v. Becker, 863 F.Supp. 2d 1190 (N.D. Ga., May 11, 2012).
18. The Copyright Clearance Center is a third-party rights management company that works on behalf of the publishers to provide permissions for a fee to individuals, universities, corporations, and so on. They do not represent all publishers.
19. Georgia State University Fair Use Check List, accessed April 10, 2014, http://www.usg.edu/copyright/fair_use_checklist/. Adapted from K. Crews and D. Buttler, "Fair Use Checklist," accessed April 10, 2014, http://copyright.columbia.edu/copyright/fair-use/fair-use-checklist/.
20. Basic Books, Inc. v. Kinko's Graphics Corporation, 758 F.Supp. 1522 (S.D.N.Y. 1991).
21. Princeton University Press v. Michigan Document Services, Inc., 99 F.3d 1381 (6th Cir. 1996), cert. denied, 520 U.S. 1156 (1997).
22. American Geophysical Union v. Texaco, Inc., 60 F.3d 913 (2d Cir. 1994), cert. dismissed, 516 U.S. 1005 (1995).
23. Agreement on Guidelines for Classroom Copying in Not-for-Profit Educational Institutions with Respect to Books and Periodicals, March 1976 (U.S. Congress, House, Copyright Law Revision, 94th Cong., 2d sess. [1976]. H. Doc. 1476; 68-70.)

24. Brandon Butler, Kenneth D. Crews, Donna Ferullo, and Kevin L. Smith, "White Paper: US Law and International Interlibrary Loan," *Research Library Issues: A Quarterly Report from ARL, CNI, and SPARC*, no. 275 (June 2011): 15–18, accessed April 10, 2014, http://publications.arl.org/rli275/.

25. Anne K. Beaubien, Marlayna Christensen, Jennifer Kuehn, David K. Larsen, and May Lehane, "White Paper: International Interlibrary Loan," *Research Library Issues: A Quarterly Report from ARL, CNI, and SPARC*, no. 275 (June 2011): 7–14, accessed April 10, 2014, http://publications.arl.org/rli275/.

26. Kirtsaeng v. John Wiley & Sons, Inc. 133 S.Ct. 1351 (2013).

27. Capitol Records, LLC v. ReDigi Inc. 934 F.Supp.2d 640 (S.S.N.Y. 2013).

28. American Library Association, "State of America's Libraries Report 2013," *American Library Association*, 2014, accessed April 8, 2014, http://www.ala.org/news/state-americas-libraries-report-2013/ebooks-and-copyright-issues. See also Lee Rainie and Maeve Duggan, *E-book Reading Jumps; Print Book Reading Declines* (Washington, DC: Pew Internet and American Life Project, 2012), accessed April 10, 2014, http://libraries.pewinternet.org/2012/12/27/e-book-reading-jumps-print-book-reading-declines/.

29. Dwayne K. Buttler, "Intimacy Gone Awry: Copyright and Special Collections," *Journal of Library Administration* 52 (2012): 279–93.

30. Salinger v. Random House, Inc. 811 F.2d 90 (2d Cir. 1987).

31. A summary judgment proceeding is one where there are no material questions of fact and one party is entitled to a ruling in their favor as a matter of law.

32. Authors Guild, Inc. v. Google, 721 F.3d 132 (2d Cir. 2013).

33. Authors Guild v. HathiTrust, 902 F.Supp2d 445 (2012).

34. Meredith Schwartz and Gary Price, "Judge's Ruling a Win for Fair Use in Authors Guild v HathiTrust Case," *Library Journal Infodocket*, October 10, 2012, accessed April 10, 2014, http://www.infodocket.com/2012/10/10/judge-rules-on-authors-guild-v-hathitrust/.

35. HathiTrust Digital Library, "Mission Goals," accessed April 9, 2014, http://www.hathitrust.org/mission_goals.

36. Google, "Company," accessed April 9, 2014, http://www.google.com/about/company/.

37. Authors Guild, Inc. v. HathiTrust, U. S. Court of Appeals for the Second Circuit, No. 12-4547 cv, June 10, 2014, accessed June 10, 2014, http://www.ca2.uscourts.gov.

38. Jennifer Howard, "HathiTrust Digital Library Wins Latest Round in Battle with Authors," *Chronicle of Higher Education*, June 10, 2014, accessed June 11, 2014, http://chronicle.com/blogs/wiredcampus/hathitrust-digital-library-wins-latest-round-in-battle-with-authors/53195.

39. Howard, 18.

40. Howard, 19.

41. Howard, 20.

42. Howard, 20.

43. Diversey v. Schmidly et al., 738 F.3d 1196 (10th Cir. 2013).

44. United States Copyright Office, *Legal Issues in Mass Digitization: A Preliminary Analysis and Discussion Document* (Washington, DC: United States Copyright Office, 2011), accessed April 10, 2014, http://www.copyright.gov/docs/massdigitization/USCOMassDigitization_October2011.pdf.

45. Michael Stebbins, "Expanding Public Access to the Results of Federally Funded Research," *U.S. Office of Science and Technology Policy* (blog), February 22, 2013, accessed April 10, 2014, http://www.whitehouse.gov/blog/2013/02/22/expanding-public-access-results-federally-funded-research.

46. Fair Access to Science and Technology Research Act of 2013, H.R. 708, 113th Cong. (2013–2014).

47. Meredith Schwartz, "ARL Launches Library-Led Solution to Federal Open Access Requirements," *Library Journal*, June 12, 2013, accessed April 10, 2014, http://lj.libraryjournal.com/2013/06/oa/arl-launches-library-led-solution-to-federal-open-access-requirements/.

48. U.S. Copyright Act, 17. U.S.C.§ 101.

49. For an in-depth treatise on licenses for libraries see Tomas Lipinski, *The Librarian's Legal Companion for Licensing Information Resources and Services* (Chicago: ALA-Neal Schuman, 2013).

# 7

## Copyright Services for Faculty

**M**ost universities still subscribe to the publish-or-perish doctrine for promotion and tenure of faculty. Besides the significant research contributions that faculty are expected to produce, they also have teaching responsibilities. As such, they are both owners of copyrighted works as well as users of copyrighted works. Both sides of that copyright coin require application of various sections of the copyright law. This chapter will address the education exceptions that faculty utilize with copyrighted materials in their teaching as well as how fair use is applied. This chapter will also cover the issues faculty encounter when entering the publishing arena.

### THE TEACHER

#### Face-to-Face Classroom Teaching

The U.S. Copyright Act provides an exception to teachers for what they can use in a face-to-face (F2F) classroom setting. Section 110(1) addresses what can be performed and displayed in the classroom. Both teachers and students are covered under this exception. Only nonprofit educational institutions are eligible to use this exception. The teaching activities can occur in a classroom setting or in a similar place devoted to instruction.

It is not unusual for professors (or students) to show movies, movie clips, or images, or play audio files that make a point or enhance the learning experience in a class. For example, a history class might show a video of *Gone with the Wind* or an art class might display slides of Impressionist paintings.

The copyright law permits such displays and performances, which are defined as the following:

> To "display" a work means to show a copy of it, either directly or by means of a film, slide, television image, or any other device or process or, in the case of a motion picture or other audiovisual work, to show individual images nonsequentially. . . .
>
> To "perform" a work means to recite, render, play, dance, or act it, either directly or by means of any device or process or, in the case of a motion picture or other audiovisual work, to show its images in any sequence or to make the sounds accompanying it audible.[1]

Under the statute, the copies that are used for the display or performance must be lawfully made. They should not be copies that have been pirated or whose origin is not known.

The copies of the works are to be used for teaching activities, whether in a classroom setting or a similar place devoted to instruction. There is much debate as to what constitutes "teaching activities" as well as "similar place devoted to instruction." The language of the statute includes a much broader concept of teaching than the traditional teacher in a classroom in a school. It recognizes that learning takes place beyond the four corners of a traditional classroom. This concept of teaching activities is very helpful by not limiting the type of learning that can happen. It does not have to be a class that is part of a university's structured curriculum.

Another key phrase in the F2F education exception is that this exception is only available to nonprofit educational institutions. There has been a meteoric rise of for-profit colleges in recent years, the most notable being the University of Phoenix. For-profit colleges are not eligible for the education exceptions and must rely on fair use.

## Distance Education

Faculty no longer confine their teaching to just the traditional classroom. Most courses are now hybrid courses with part of the course being F2F and the other part utilizing an online component generally known as a course management system (CMS). It is believed that this model provides a more robust learning environment for the students by providing direct access to course materials and opportunities to participate in group discussions. The copyright issues arise with the placement of copyrighted materials on the CMS.

The second part of the education exception, section 110(2), addresses online teaching or what is more commonly known as distance education.

This section of the copyright law was amended in 2002 and is the Technology, Education and Copyright Harmonization Act commonly referred to as TEACH. The previous version was not flexible and only allowed for synchronous education in which the students gathered in one place at one time, where they received the broadcast. TEACH allows for asynchronous education, but there are many requirements that must be met before one can avail oneself of the exception.

TEACH is applicable to the digital transmission of works. It is similar to the F2F exception in that it is divided into what can be performed and displayed. The definitions remain the same, but by the very nature of it being a digital transmission, the application is different. TEACH allows for works to be displayed but only in an amount that would be displayed in an F2F classroom setting. For example, in an art class, a professor might show slides of famous paintings or art works but only a small number due to the time constraints of the class. In a digital asynchronous environment, it is possible to display or post an unlimited number of slides easier and faster, and many times the digital copy is much cleaner than one that has been reproduced to show in a classroom. However, although the format lends itself to a digital classroom, the professor must only show a number of images that would be comparable to a live classroom setting.

Under TEACH performances are limited to non-dramatic literary or musical works or reasonable and limited portions of other works such as dramatic works. A non-dramatic literary or musical work would include fiction, poetry, and short stories but does not include audiovisual works. A non-dramatic musical work would include most music but would exclude operas, musicals, and music videos. Non-dramatic works can be performed in their entirety. The statute restricts the performance of dramatic works to reasonable and limited portions. This allows for flexibility in what is needed for the course. However, it is also difficult to determine what Congress meant by "reasonable and limited portions" and to date no court has defined the meaning of the phrase.

Before one can take advantage of the exception there are institutional and technological requirements that must be met as well as restrictions on the professor's responsibilities and the type of materials that can be used. If the requirements cannot be met, then the exception is not available to the professor. K–12 schools are also eligible for this exception if they meet the requirements.

An institution must be accredited and nonprofit. It must have a copyright policy and provide copyright information to faculty, students, and relevant staff. The university is also responsible for providing notice to students that the works that are used in the course may be subject to copyright protection.

Many schools cannot meet this first hurdle, since they might not have a copyright policy in place. If they do have a policy, then they are also responsible for providing copyright information to their constituency. Questions arise as to what type of copyright information is required and sufficient and how that information should be distributed to the parties as defined under the statute. Is a website sufficient or does each individual person need to receive the information directly? Is the onus upon the individuals to seek out the information, or should it be handed/delivered to them? The law is vague, which allows for flexibility in how each institution meets the requirements. Students also must be informed that the materials that are being transmitted to them may be protected by copyright. How does a university meet that requirement? Some provide a standard statement on their course management system, while others provide the copyright statement on the selected materials. It must also be noted that the F2F classroom exception specifies that only nonprofit educational institutions can utilize that part of the statute. Congress took it one step further for distance education and also required that the educational institution be accredited as well as nonprofit.

There are also technological requirements that must be in place before the TEACH exception can be invoked. The institution must have technology in place that can reasonably prevent the recipients/students from retaining the work longer than the class session as well as further distributing it. This is generally known as controlling downstream distribution. Access to the materials must be restricted to only those students enrolled in the course. If the copyright holder has placed any technological measures on the work that prevent dissemination and retention, then those measures cannot be interfered with.

The types of materials that can be transmitted are narrow in scope. No works that are produced or marketed primarily for education can be used. The concern here was that textbooks would be digitized and transmitted, thereby severely impacting the market for the work. The materials that can be used would be considered more supplementary in nature. They would be works that are not produced just for the educational market but have a broader audience. The works allowed under TEACH must be directly related to the course content and the educator must use only what he or she would have used in an F2F setting. If there is no digital version of the work available, then the work can be digitized but only the amount that is needed to accomplish the educational goals. Posted works must be under the supervision of the instructor. Students are certainly allowed to post as well, but the instructor must have some control over what is posted. Instructors should not be just passive bystanders but be fully aware of what works are being transmitted for their course.

TEACH is very restrictive because the content holders were quite concerned that allowing works to be posted in the online environment would severely impact their revenue stream. However, there is also language in the act, consistent with the rest of the copyright law, that requires a "reasonable" effort. It does not demand an absolute assurance. Throughout many areas of law, there is the "reasonable person" concept, which basically requires that the situation be assessed through the eyes of the average person. The Copyright Act follows this legal precedent.

Due to the many restrictions and qualifications of TEACH, educators will sometimes bypass this exception and utilize fair use instead. It is certainly understandable that educators would not want to attempt to apply such a complex section of the statute, but it is advisable to take advantage of every exception allowed under the law. Sometimes the best strategy is to analyze the use that is needed and apply all available options such as both fair use and the education exceptions.

**Fair Use**

With the passage of the 1976 Copyright Act, came the Classroom Guidelines.[2] They were part of a House Report on how educators could apply fair use in the classroom. The Classroom Guidelines are not legally binding, but many educators believe that they are and attempt to frame their fair-use argument under the rubric of the guidelines.

The most often quoted part of the guidelines describes when a teacher can make multiple copies of a work to distribute to the students. The copying must meet the brevity and spontaneity test as well as the cumulative effect test.

Brevity qualifies the amount of different types of works that can be copied and distributed to the students. For example, 250 words from a poem and 1,000 words or 10 percent of a work of prose, whichever is less. The spontaneity test requires that the teacher decide on the use of a work so close in time to the start of the class that there is no opportunity to obtain permission from the copyright holder to use the work in the classroom. The cumulative effect test limits the number of times such on-the-spot copying can occur. For example, only one article or excerpt from the same author can be used in the same term and only nine instances of spontaneous copying is allowed during the term.

It is important to debunk the myth that the 1976 Classroom Guidelines are part of the U.S. Copyright Act. The actual law has no such restrictions. As stated in previous chapters, Section 107 is the fair-use section of the law and that is the language that should be applied in a fair-use analysis. The fair-use clause specifically states that it is fair use to make multiple copies for classroom use. There are no percentages attached to this statement, nor is there any requirement that it must be a last-minute decision on the part of the educator to use the work. The clause also does not require that the works be only print based. There is no format that is specified that allows the potential use and distribution of digital works as well.

Following are some of the common questions on teaching that copyright officers address.

*Can professors show movies to their classes?* On the surface this appears to be a very simple and straightforward question. However, there are multiple layers to this question. First, is it in an F2F classroom setting, or is it being delivered online? The second immediate question that needs to be determined is if the copy that will be used is a lawfully made copy under the law and if there are any restrictions on its use.

In an F2F classroom setting, at one time it would have been a VHS tape or a DVD that had either been borrowed from the library or that the professor had purchased that was then used on school-owned equipment available in the classrooms. At times, professors would bring in VHS tapes or DVDs that had been rented from stores such as Blockbuster. This can still certainly be the case, but as more delivery options present themselves, the older model of showing films is not quite as prevalent. The more common scenario is that the film is available through Netflix, iTunes, Amazon, or some other similar vendor. If this is the case, then they did not purchase a copy of the movie to own but purchased a license to use it under certain conditions. One must read the license terms quite carefully to determine if showing the movie in a classroom is allowable. The terms of use generally require that the work be used for personal, noncommercial use.

If the movie is to be delivered online to the students, then a whole other set of questions presents itself. If the movie is from one of the vendors described above, then one must look to the terms of the license to determine use. If the movie is in a VHS or DVD format, then there is a conversion that has to happen in order for the movie to be shown online or streamed. The digital file that is made might or might not be a lawfully made copy under the U.S. Copyright Act. There is a section of the copyright law that prohibits the circumvention of technological devices to access copyrighted works. This part of the law is known as the Digital Millennium Copyright Act (DMCA) and was passed in 1998. There have been some exemptions of classes of works that have been carved out that will be discussed below, but many times there is a dispute as to whether the converted copy is a lawfully made one. It is incumbent upon the educator to review the requirements for the distance education exception, aka TEACH Act, and/or the fair-use exception to determine if the copy is lawfully made and if it can be used. Under TEACH, an analog version can be converted to a digital version, but only reasonable and limited portions can be transmitted. There is no definition of "reasonable and limited" in the law, so unless a university or school system has coined a definition, then it is an analysis that must be done by the educator. How much of the movie is truly needed to accomplish the course objective? It might only need to be one or two scenes to demonstrate a point. It is up to the educator to make that determination. However, one must remember that the educator and the university or school system must also comply with the other TEACH requirements noted above, such as distribution only to students enrolled in the course.

If the educator needs to use the entire movie, then looking at the fair-use exception might be a better option. The four-factor test needs to be applied, just as it would in any other situation. The first factor would generally weigh in favor of fair use, since the purpose is educational. If the movie is more along the lines of a documentary rather than a mega-hit, then the nature of the work would favor fair use. The amount factor is always one of the trickier parts of fair use. However, the educator must look at how much of the movie is truly needed. If it is the entire work, then the amount would certainly be large but could potentially still weigh in favor of fair use. Educators are not restricted in this factor to "reasonable and limited" amounts as dictated under TEACH. More often than not there is no market impact under the fourth fair-use factor, particularly if there is restricted access to the movie and the movie was legally purchased by the library or the university. Depending upon the specific responses to each factor, fair use might be the best option for the online delivery of an entire movie to a class.

In 2012, the University of California at Los Angeles (UCLA) won the lawsuit brought against it by Ambrose Publishing, Inc., and the Association for Information Media and Equipment (AIME) for streaming copyrighted video.[3] Ambrose and AIME claimed that the UCLA streaming of copyrighted video for faculty and students to use in courses was an infringement of copyright. UCLA defended their use by claiming that the streaming was a legal use under fair use and TEACH.

Under the DMCA, the Librarian of Congress is required to make determinations every three years as to what classes of works should be exempt from DMCA restrictions. The caveat is that the exemptions are only valid for the three years unless renewed by the Librarian. In the most recent round of rulemaking in 2012, the Librarian has approved both university professors and K–12 teachers to circumvent the technology on DVDs and online sources to extract excerpts of movies for commentary and criticism.

If the use is outside of the terms of use that accompany online movies or the copyright law exceptions, then two options remain. The educator can seek permission from the copyright holder to use the work in the online environment or require the students to purchase the movie.

*How can professors legally distribute journal articles to the students in their classes?* In an F2F classroom setting, a professor can display an article under section 110(1). More than likely though, fair use would be the exception of choice, since it specifically states that it is a fair use to make multiple copies for classroom use. It is important to note, however, that this is a distribution of a single article and not multiple articles compiled by the professor into a course pack. A compilation of articles could be considered a new work with a separate copyright.

If the educator wants to post the journal article online, then they would have to see if TEACH, fair use, or both would apply. The first question that needs to be addressed is where did they get the copy? If it is a journal article from a database that the library has a license for, then the best way to distribute the article to the students is to post a link to it. Educators try to make it easier for the students by posting a PDF of the article. However, it is far preferable to post a link. If it is not possible to post a link, then access to the PDF of the article should be restricted to only the students in the class and should not be available longer than is necessary.

*How can professors legally distribute book chapters to students in their classes?* In an F2F classroom setting, an educator should look at the application of fair use. In an online setting both TEACH and fair use could potentially apply. One of the dilemmas in applying fair use is the amount factor. The age-old question is how much is too much? An approach to this is for the educator to determine what is needed to accomplish the course objectives. If the fair-use argument is being made in an Eleventh Circuit state (Georgia, Florida, or Alabama), then one should look at the Georgia State University case for guidance. If TEACH is the defense of choice, then the educator must only use materials that are not produced for the educational market and are more supplementary in nature. They also need to be cognizant of the TEACH requirement that allows them to only use amounts comparable to what they would have used in an F2F setting. Regardless of the arena and method of delivery, it is generally not acceptable to distribute or post chapters of a textbook or other book week by week or periodically until the whole work has been copied in order to bypass having the students purchase the work.

## THE RESEARCHER

Educators not only teach but generally have research responsibilities, requirements, and interests. They transition from using copyrighted works in the classroom to using copyrighted works for their research and to being the copyright owner of creative works. Understanding copyright ownership issues is critical for educators to make informed decisions and to manage their copyrights in a way that will allow them the most success in their career.

An issue that researchers are frequently encountering and one that has become quite common is the inability to locate or identify the owner of copyrighted works that they would like to use in their publications. These works are known as orphan works. As the duration of copyright becomes increasingly longer, as more publishers merge or go out of business, and with the explosion of online works, the researcher can become bogged down trying to locate the copyright owner to seek permission to incorporate parts of their work into a new work. The U.S. Copyright Office identified this issue as one that Congress needs to address and conducted a study in 2006.[4] The Copyright Office made recommendations to Congress that would reduce the liability on users of orphan works if the copyright owner should come forward, provided that the user had done due diligence in trying to locate the copyright owner. Orphan works legislation was introduced in 2006 and 2008 but neither was ever signed into law. As of this writing, no orphan works legislation is pending in Congress.

The first question that educators must ask themselves about the works they create is: Who owns the copyright? If they are employed by a university, they need to determine if there is a university policy regarding ownership of works created at their institution. Most businesses follow the work-for-hire doctrine, which means that works created by employees as part of their employment belong to the employer. However, many universities have taken the step of granting faculty the right to retain ownership of the copyrighted works created at their institution. Intellectual property ownership policies can vary widely, however. Some allow faculty to retain copyright in all the works they create, while others place conditions on certain types of works. For example, many institutions allow faculty to own the copyright in traditional works of scholarship such as books, textbooks, and journal articles. They might also allow ownership of instructional copyrightable material such as syllabi. Restrictions usually revolve around online courses and course materials. In recent years there have been revisions in intellectual property policies to reflect the ever-changing educational environment. One of the changes is a caveat to the faculty ownership of copyrights. Some policies provide the university with a nonexclusive license to use faculty works for educational, promotional, and research purposes. The nonexclusive license gives the university flexibility in using the works in a limited way without constantly seeking faculty permission. Faculty still retain copyright ownership but subject to the conditions of the nonexclusive license.

Another reason for the inclusion of the grant of nonexclusive licenses by faculty to the universities is part of the groundswell of open-access initiatives across many campuses. As university budgets tighten, and with that the domino effect of fewer university dollars going to fund library collections, the traditional model of faculty retaining copyright ownership of works they create at their institutions was revisited. The university pays faculty to research and to disseminate their research findings. Faculty generally give their copyright to publishers in exchange for being published and then universities have to buy back the intellectual output that they initially paid for. It is a boon for publishers but it has serious financial implications for shrinking university budgets. The open-access movement attempts to somewhat shift control from publishers back to the universities and their faculty. Open-access policies are generally separate from intellectual property policies, but both dictate ownership and use of faculty copyrights.

Once a determination has been made as to the initial copyright ownership and conditions thereof, then the researcher has to consider the implications of joint authorship, publishing options, and sharing their research. In today's academy it is quite typical to have more than one author for a journal article. There are copyright implications as to rights when two or more authors join together to create a work. Under the U.S. Copyright Act the authors must have the intent at the time of writing to merge their work.[5] It is not something that they can decide at a later date. If there are any profits earned from the sale or license of the work, then there must be an accounting to all co-owners. Generally, it is decided at the beginning of the joint effort as to the percentage of the royalties each author will receive. Each individual author may enter into a nonexclusive license with a third party without the knowledge or consent of the co-owners. It is only when the author wants to provide a third party with an exclusive license that all authors must agree, since an exclusive license restricts all authors' use of the work.

In the academic setting the old adage of "publish or perish" is still alive and well. Untenured assistant professors need to have published articles in peer-reviewed journals in order to receive tenure and promotion to associate professor. To achieve the rank of full professor, some disciplines require publication of a book in addition to journal articles.

Whether it is a journal article or a book, authors enter into agreements with publishers, and copyright is at the heart of the agreements. The agreement is a contract between the author and publisher and it dictates the terms of what each party is responsible for. The issue of copyright ownership is generally handled differently with book contracts vs. journal article contracts.

For book contracts the standard is for authors to transfer their copyright to the publisher in exchange for having their work published and generally receive royalties calculated on the number of books sold. Books generally will hold their value for a longer period of time than a journal article and remain in the market in various formats, which is one of the reasons why the publishers require the transfer. This is particularly seen in the publication of textbooks.

Journal article contracts are different in that the publisher may require the author to transfer copyright in exchange for having their work published but there is a bit more flexibility in negotiating terms that are more favorable to the author. Unlike book contracts, journal article contracts do not involve any type of payment to the author.

It's always recommended that authors negotiate their contracts with the publisher. Once the author transfers their copyright, then they no longer have any rights to their work except what is agreed to in the contract. Authors need to consider the uses they want to make of their own work, such as posting on their website or their institutional repository, using their work for future research, and sharing their work with colleagues. There are standard addenda that can be attached to a contract that specify the rights that will be retained by an author. It's not unusual to have an embargo period of six to twelve months, which gives the publisher exclusive control over the work during that time but then the rights the author negotiated can go into effect after the embargo period. The Committee on Institutional Cooperation (CIC) is a consortium of the Big Ten universities and has an addendum[6] that can be used by authors; there is also one distributed by the Scholarly Publishing and Academic Resources Coalition (SPARC).[7]

The traditional publishing model described above is slowly changing as new publishing models are developed. The open-access initiative has given rise to open-access options. Some commercial publishers will offer authors the option to pay to have their article available to open access. The cost to the author can be thousands of dollars. This allows the publisher to recoup the cost of the publishing services associated with the publication, marketing, and sale of the journal article. However, there is controversy over how acceptable this is in the eyes of the academy and whether or not the university and not the author should pay the fees. Some institutions have established funds to cover the cost, while others are grappling with the implications to university and library budgets.

Federal grants are a big business for universities. In FY 2011, the U.S. government shelled out $40 billion to universities for research and development.[8] As part of the promotion and tenure process, universities take into account how many grants the researcher has obtained. As discussed in earlier chapters, the federal government is considering open-access policies similar to the one developed by NIH. This impacts the scope of the agreement that the researcher can enter into with a publisher. Generally, the requirement for the recipients of an NIH grant is that any peer-reviewed journal article that is a result of the grant must be deposited into PubMed Central within twelve months of publication. Other federal agencies will more than likely have a similar requirement. Researchers must be aware of these requirements and take them into account when negotiating publication agreements. If they do not comply with the federal agency dictates, then there is the very real likelihood that they will lose the grant funding and their university would be subject to similar sanctions. The stakes are high, so researchers have to be cognizant of the rules and must not sign agreements that would put themselves or their universities at risk of losing federal funding.

Another twist is that in 2011, the National Science Foundation (NSF) required that researchers submit data management plans as part of their grant proposals. Other federal agencies that are looking at instituting open-access policies are also considering adding an open-access data component. Universities are responding in different ways to the NSF mandate. For example, Purdue University created the Purdue University Research Repository (PURR), which provides a platform to organize and manage data. It was a joint collaboration between the Libraries, Information Technology, and the Office of the VP for Research. The Libraries also developed a data management plan toolkit to assist researchers in identifying the data issues and address how to manage the data according to the federal agency requirements. Copyright plays a part in data management as well. Raw data is generally not protectable under the U.S. Copyright Act since they are basically facts. However, the compilation and arrangement of the data could result in a copyrightable work. So much of the data in open access is uncharted territory. The full impact of copyright related issues is yet to be realized.

In addition to attempting to reduce the buyback of material already paid for with faculty salaries, open access also allows more collaboration across borders. Faculty at institutions within the United States not only join together on research projects but bring in partners from all over the world. There are copyright laws in just about every country of the world. As discussed in previous chapters, the Berne Convention and WIPO controls and dictates much of the use and determines which country's law will apply in a conflict. The United States is also part of the Universal Copyright Convention, which recognizes the copyright laws of member nations. The United States is also party to many bilateral agreements with specific countries that act similarly to Berne and UCC. It can become quite complex to determine which laws will apply in any given situation. The important thing to note is that if a researcher contemplates collaborating with a non-U.S. citizen, then it is in everyone's best interests to determine which country's copyright laws might apply and the benefits and disadvantages to each of them.

The following questions by faculty are typically addressed by a university copyright office.

*Who owns my course?* To respond to this question one must determine what exactly is a course and what truly concerns the faculty member. Courses can consist of syllabi, professor's notes, lectures, PowerPoint presentations, and so forth. They can be taught in the traditional F2F classroom setting. They could be a hybrid with part of it taught F2F and the other through a course management system or they could be taught totally online. It is important for the faculty member to distinguish what specifically he or she needs information on and then look for guidance to the intellectual property policy of their institution. Copyright generally resides with the faculty in their lecture notes and any PowerPoint presentation that they developed.

Issues have arisen in recent years as to the copyrightability of lecture notes due to the development of commercial note-taking businesses. Companies hire students typically enrolled in the class to take notes from the lectures and then the company posts those notes online and charges students fees to access them. The dispute has arisen as to who owns the notes that the students take during the class—the professor or the student. If it is copying verbatim what the professor has written on a blackboard or distributed, then the copyright is certainly with the professor. However, the question remains if the student then interprets the information that the professor has provided, is it a derivative work owned by the professor or is it a new work with the copyright being owned by the student? In such situations, each case needs to be looked at individually to determine the specific facts. Some schools have directly addressed this issue by adopting policies that specifically prohibit students from participating in commercial note-taking ventures.

The distribution of potentially copyrighted faculty material does not stop with note-taking companies but has expanded far beyond that. There are companies that again pay students to post exams, papers, case studies, math problems, and so on. If the university has allowed the faculty to retain their copyright in such works, then it is up to the faculty to choose whether or not to vigorously defend their copyrights.

Students are quite inventive in how they capture the intellectual output of a course. They can take pictures from their cell phones of materials posted in the classroom and can also videotape a professor's lecture. Students should obtain permission from the professor before commencing any videotaping. However, the copyright in the videotape would belong to the student, who then might choose to use it in a way that could potentially infringe on faculty or university copyright. Many faculty place restrictions on what is allowed and post those restrictions on their syllabi. Acceptance of the restrictions is a condition of enrollment for the class.

Copyright does attach to syllabi, but some universities will claim a non-exclusive license to use the syllabi for a certain number of years. This is to provide the university the opportunity to continue the course should the professor die or leave the institution. The professor retains copyright and can still use the work in whatever way he or she chooses. This is also a very typical scenario for online courses, particularly for ones that have been videotaped.

*Who owns my data?* Researchers can produce massive amounts of data during the course of their professional careers. Universities are developing repositories to store the data for an average period of ten years. There are data management collection policies that are under development to determine how to weed out the data that is no longer necessary to retain and what is a reasonable amount of time to keep the data. In order to have that flexibility and also to comply with many other laws dealing with data submissions, most universities retain ownership of the data. There is usually a separate data policy from the intellectual property policy but the researcher should be aware of the requirements for data at his or her institution.

*Since I wrote the article, then I should be able to post it on my website or do what I want with it; isn't that correct?* If the article was published by a commercial or society publisher rather than self-published, then faculty need to review the contract that they signed with the publisher to determine what rights they might have retained. Once the copyright is transferred to the publisher, then the author no longer has any rights in the work unless they negotiated some. If they want to post to an unrestricted website an article that they wrote but no longer have any rights to, then they need to obtain permission from the publisher.

*I want to include part of a work by another author in a work that I am creating, but I can't find the author to seek permission. What are my options?* This is a classic orphan works issue, where the author cannot be identified and/or located. One of the first steps is to try to contact the publisher of the work if it is still in business, since more than likely the author transferred the copyright to the publisher. If the publisher is defunct or merged with another publishing company and cannot ascertain whether its inventory contains the asset, then the faculty member might want to contact the author, who might have more information. It could be possible that the author retained the copyright or at least some rights that he or she might be able to share. If neither of those scenarios pans out, then the faculty member might want to consider substituting something that is similar where the permission can be obtained. If that is not an option, then should the faculty member move forward and use the work, he or she would be assuming liability for a potentially infringing use. Many times publishers will not take that risk, but if the faculty member is willing to assume it, the publisher might draft language in the publishing contract to that effect.

*What copyright issues should I be thinking about when entering into a publishing agreement?* The first consideration is to determine whether or not the faculty member has the legal right to enter into the agreement. Does the university allow faculty to retain their copyright to the type of work that is under consideration for publication? If so, are there any conditions on that right? Many open-access policies grant the university a nonexclusive license to faculty works. If this is the case, then a contract cannot be signed that provides the publisher with an exclusive license or a transfer of copyright, since there is a restriction on that right by the university. Faculty need to carefully read all the terms of the contract to ensure that they can comply with them.

*What copyright issues should I be thinking about when applying for a grant?* It's always important to understand the grant requirements regarding publication and retention of copyright. Does the grant specify who owns the copyright to the work? Is it the granting agency, the university, or the researchers? Are there restrictions on any works produced as a result of the grant? NIH requires that certain types of works must be deposited into PubMed Central, a repository of biomedical literature, within twelve months of publication. If this is the requirement, then authors cannot sign publishing agreements that do not allow them to make that deposit. There are some publishers who understand the restrictions placed on the researchers and will make the deposit for them. If this is the case, it should all be spelled out in the contract.

*How do I determine which journals/publishers are author friendly?* There is a database called Sherpa/Romeo that lists publishers' copyright policies. It is a good place to check to see how friendly they are to authors in terms of the rights they allow authors to retain. Some will allow authors to retain copyright but provide them with a license to publish. Some will allow authors to post their final manuscript to the author's institutional repository but not the final published version. Some publishers are very restrictive and will not provide the author with any rights whatsoever. The database is a good place to begin searching for an appropriate venue for the author's research, but it is only the beginning step. It is always recommended for authors to discuss concerns with the publisher to determine if they can come to some agreement.

## CONCLUSION

Educators, be they teachers, researchers, or both, encounter copyright issues every day. The copyright law has carved out exceptions for teachers for F2F and the online environment. The exceptions certainly have some flexibility to them but also require the educator to be familiar with the restrictions. Fair use is also applicable to works that are used in the classroom as well as works produced by the educator. However, the argument that all educational use is fair use is inaccurate. Educational use is but one component of the four-factor fair-use test. It is in the best interest of the educator to understand the options that are available to them as well as the associated risks.

## NOTES

1. U.S. Copyright Act, 17. U.S.C.§ 101.

2. Agreement on Guidelines for Classroom Copying in Not-For-Profit Educational Institutions with Respect to Books and Periodicals (Copyright Law Revision, 94th Cong., 2d sess. [1976]. H.R Doc. No. 1476, at 68–70).

3. Association for Information Media and Equipment v. Regents of the University of California, No. CV 10-9378 CBM (MANx) (C.D. Cal. Oct. 3, 2011). 2012 U.S. Dist. LEXIS 187811 (C.D. Cal. Nov. 20, 2012).

4. United States Copyright Office, *Report on Orphan Works* (Washington, DC: Library of Congress, 2006), accessed April 10, 2014, http://www.copyright.gov/orphan/orphan-report.pdf.

5. U.S. Copyright Act, 17. U.S.C.§ 101.

6. Committee on Institutional Cooperation, "CIC Author's Addendum Brochure," accessed April 9, 2014, http://www.cic.net/projects/library/scholarly-communication/authors-addendum-brochure.

7. Scholarly Publishing and Academic Resources Coalition, "Author's Rights: The SPARC Author Addendum," 2013, accessed April 10, 2014, http://www.sparc.arl.org/initiatives/author-rights.

8. "10 Universities that Receive the Most Government Money: 24/7 Wall Street," *Huffington Post* (blog), April 29, 2013, accessed April 10, 2014, http://www.huffington post.com/2013/04/27/universities-government-money_n_3165186.html.

# 8

## Copyright Services for Administrators and Staff

Copyright issues have a broad reach across a university. It is not only faculty and students that must navigate the maze that is copyright but also staff at all levels from clerical to senior level administrators. This chapter will look at the various departments and issues that a copyright officer handles on any given day.

### STUDENT SERVICES

The start of an academic year brings thousands of freshmen to campuses all across the country. Most institutions have orientations for new students at the beginning of the fall semester that range from a day to a week. The orientations introduce them to the campus and the services provided and put them on notice as to their rights and responsibilities as students. Since there is an incredible amount of information that needs to be distributed to the students during the orientation, there is usually only a small amount of time allotted to departments to present their information. However, this is a wonderful opportunity to at least introduce copyright. Many times the copyright piece is combined with the rules for using university computers and the university network, but at least it can be a start to a conversation. If the freshmen can at least remember that the issue was raised during orientation and associate a person with it, then it is a success. The details can come at a later time.

The Dean of Students Office is an excellent resource and support to students. A partnership between that office and the copyright office is incredibly beneficial to all. Generally, the Dean of Students Office regulates and advises student organizations. It's a real boon for a copyright office to have a direct line of communication through the dean's office to the organizations. Copyright becomes an issue during student-sponsored programs and events, whether it's a movie night or designing posters using copyrighted images to advertise a fund-raiser.

One of the issues that also arises with student organizations and student-run programs is the legal relationship between the student organizations and the university. Are the student organizations a legal entity on their own, or are they tied into the university? There are clear-cut obligations that employers must meet for their employees, but student organizations can be somewhere in the middle. It's important to clarify their legal relationship with the university in case any of their activities result in legal action. Another consideration for the copyright officer who is an employee of the university is that person's role in advising these organizations. Since this is an educational environment, the provision of legal information is usually encouraged.

Another area that a Dean of Students Office can be responsible for is drafting, implementing, and enforcing a student honor code. Sometimes an honor code can include a segment on copyright. It can provide a brief overview and then refer the student to campus resources on copyright. The goal is to make the students aware of their responsibility in that area and encourage them to respect copyright.

Following are two typical examples of questions received by a copyright officer in conjunction with the Dean of Students Office's activities and responsibilities.

*Can a student organization show a movie?* Many student organizations show movies for a variety of purposes. If it is a movie that is being shown for entertainment purposes to anyone who shows up at the door, then the organization must obtain a public performance license. There are companies such as Movie Licensing USA that can provide such a license for a fee. There is a misconception that if the student organization does not charge a fee, then they do not need the public performance license. This is inaccurate. The issue is that the movie is being shown to a broader group than just a small number of family and friends, and it has no other purpose than just entertainment. However, if the organization is showing the movie for educational purposes, then section 110(1) of the U.S. Copyright Act allows such use for "F2F teaching activities of a nonprofit educational institution in a classroom or similar place devoted to instruction." There could be the occasion where a professor has been asked to lead a group discussion on the movie topic. Fair use might also apply in this situation. Even though an exception can apply, administrators might require that the student organization obtain a public performance license to ensure that neither the students nor the institution incurs any liability. A lawfully made copy of the movie must be used no matter what exception is claimed.

*The film club is sponsoring a video contest with an Oscar-like premiere of the winning videos shown at a local theater. What are the copyright issues that the club will need to address?* The club needs to ensure that all entrants have the appropriate copyright authority to show their video in public. The video entries might have been created for another purpose, such as a class project where fair use could apply, but once it has been removed from the classroom, then potentially permissions might be needed for a public performance. The club might also consider having the creator of the videos sign a release that they are in compliance with all applicable laws and that they are legally competent to enter into such an agreement. It should be decided at the beginning if there will be any streaming of the videos or if they will only be viewed by the attendees at the theater. There can be additional copyright issues every time there is greater access to the videos. The club also needs to ensure that any agreements they sign with a theater or similar venue details who will assume liability for violation of any laws.

## ADMINISTRATIVE ISSUES

### Printing Services

There are some educational institutions that provide copy/printing services. Some have separate copy shops and others are incorporated into libraries or various units or departments. Some institutions have outsourced all of their duplication services. Copy services departments generally provide a multitude of copying options ranging from compiling course packs to designing brochures and posters to market events on campus. Most university printing operations are on a cost-recovery basis. They are generally self-sustaining entities but are not for-profit enterprises. For those institutions that still retain a copy shop or provide such services, they have to be diligent in addressing copyright issues.

Campus copy shops produce course packs for faculty. They can be print or digital but each format raises copyright concerns. There has been course pack litigation as described in previous chapters with both the Kinko's and Michigan Document Services cases. Both of those cases involved commercial copy shops. To date, there has been no litigation against an in-house copy shop at a university.

If it is a print course pack, many printing services departments require permissions to print and will not rely on fair use. It is common practice to have the department utilize the services of the Copyright Clearance Center, which is a third-party rights management company, to obtain permission from the publishers to reprint journal articles, book chapters, and so on for a fee. The royalties are calculated into the total sale price of the course pack. This has become a fairly straightforward transaction. What has become more complicated are digital course packs where the rights issues are not as transparent as print. With digital course packs questions abound as to the origin of the material and any restrictions on the use of such material:

1. Is the material being scanned by a printing services employee, or is the digital scan being provided? If the employee is doing the scanning, then where/how did they obtain the print copy? Did a professor provide the print copy? If so, does the professor have to sign any type of release or waiver stating that the copy is a lawfully made copy?
2. Did printing services staff contact the rights holder for permission to scan? If so, then there could be times where the rights holder already has a digital copy available so that no scanning is required.
3. If the digital copy is being provided, then how was it obtained? Is the digital copy part of a database that the libraries have a subscription to? If so, then the terms of use are governed by the contract between the libraries/university and the rights holder and needs to be reviewed. Some rights holders specifically state in their contracts that use for digital course packs are allowed but with some restrictions.

Printing services departments also provide duplication services for many other items than course packs. It could be a copy of a journal article, class lecture notes, cartoon strip, or any of several other types of works that are protected by copyright. Does the department have policies on what they will duplicate and how they will make such determinations? For example, will they require any customer who asks them to make a copy of a copyrighted work, where the customer does not own the copyright in the work, to sign a release form stating that they will assume all liability? Does the department actively engage in providing copyright information to its customers including some type of fair-use analysis checklist? University copy shops are not immune from liability, so it is important that the staff understand what is at stake and have appropriate policies to ensure compliance with the U.S. Copyright Act.

**Campus Entertainment Services**

Campus productions of concerts, plays, and art exhibits require close scrutiny by administrators to ensure that they are in compliance with the copyright law. It is well understood that any public performances of copyrighted plays and music require payment of a licensing fee. However, applying the copyright law to music and sound recordings can be confusing. "A composition and the recording of it are distinct and separate copyrightable works, with independent originality and fixation. The recorded performance of the composition becomes a sound recording and enjoys copyright protection independent of the copyright in the underlying musical work."[1] A sound recording might not include any music. It could be a recording of Martin Luther King's "I Have a Dream" speech. Music is generally comprised of the musical composition as well as the performance of the composition.

To use any of these works requires licenses from several organizations. "For historical reasons, principally the advent of radio and television broadcasting, the performance of nondramatic musical works has been of growing importance to broadcasters and to copyright owners who ultimately devised licensing collectives to clear permission rights and to allocate requisite royalties to copyright holders."[2] If the performance is going to be videotaped, then there is a synchronization license that is needed as well.

The good news is that most universities have blanket licenses with the performing rights societies that control the copyright for the performances such as BMI, ASCAP, SESAC, and the Harry Fox Licensing Agency. These agencies represent the rights of the copyright holders. Blanket licenses provide the rules for using the works that are in the agency's inventory and allow the university to use the works without requesting permission or paying a royalty for each use. The licenses are generally for several years and the university pays one fee for the term of the license. The fee can be based upon the number of full-time students enrolled at the institution. However, it is important to verify that the university does indeed have such licenses and that the works used for the productions are managed by the performance rights societies. If the works are not part of the inventories, then permissions must be sought from the individual copyright holders, which can be an expensive and laborious process.

A companion issue is that such productions, including sporting events, are generally videotaped and used for multiple purposes. The trend now is to digitize those videotapes and post them on both internal and external websites. There are layers of copyright issues that must be addressed before this can happen. For example, at sporting events music is played in the venue at different times throughout the event. The school band can also be playing musical compositions during halftime. During the sporting event there can also be background videos playing on jumbotrons. There are potential copyrights in each of those works as well as in the video. Also consider any arrangements with either local or network television or radio stations. The contracts with such media organizations will dictate the copyright terms. Any other related contracts and licenses must be revisited to determine if the digitization is allowed as well as making the digitized versions publicly available.

**Information Technology Services**

Illegal downloading and sharing of copyrighted materials particularly by students is quite common at universities. The Digital Millennium Copyright Act of 1998 (DMCA)[3] gives universities the opportunity to self-identify as Internet service providers (ISP) and by doing so avoid liability for the alleged infringement of copyrighted works being posted on their networks. This is both a blessing and a challenge for university administrators, particularly in information technology departments, who are charged with maintaining a secure network. The DMCA recognizes that ISPs only host the networks but do not control the actual works that are being downloaded, shared, posted, and stored on those networks. They are considered only a conduit. However, universities do have a responsibility under the DMCA to remove any allegedly infringing material once they are notified that it has been located on their network. This can be a complex and labor-intensive procedure. Below are some of the questions that usually arise with DMCA complaints.

*What is a DMCA notice?* A DMCA notice is sent by the copyright owner to the owner of the server/network informing the network/server that the copyright owner's material has been found on the server and it has been posted without permission. The notice is referred to as a takedown notice and requires the institution to take down the allegedly infringing work. Under the law, the notice must adhere to a certain format and contain very specific information, such as what work was downloaded and when. If the notice does not meet the requirements, then the university is under no legal obligation to respond. However, for all practical purposes, universities will generally address the notice and proceed with the takedown or notify the copyright owner of the problem with the notice.

*What is the procedure when a university receives a DMCA notice?* As required under the DMCA, ISPs register the name of their DMCA agent with the U.S. Copyright Office. Complaints of copyright infringement of materials found on a university server are usually sent to the agent, who has an e-mail address in the IT department that has been set up for that particular purpose. The notice does not identify the user by name but by an Internet protocol (IP) address. Such addresses are usually assigned to specific computers. Universities can then track the owner/user of the computer through the IP address. Wireless networks make the identification process a bit more difficult, but a person can still be identified. Once the identification has occurred, then the allegedly infringing material must be removed from the network. This can happen in a variety of ways but is usually a coordinated effort between central and departmental IT units, Dean of Students Office, and administrators in deans' offices. Often once the material has been removed or taken down no further legal action is taken.

## DMCA TAKEDOWN NOTICE

The DMCA requires that all infringement claims must be in writing and must include the following information:

1. A physical or electronic signature of the copyright owner or the person authorized to act on the owner's behalf;
2. A description of the copyrighted work claimed to have been infringed;
3. A description of the infringing material and information reasonably sufficient to permit the material to be located;
4. Your contact information, including your mailing address, telephone number, and e-mail;
5. A statement by you that you have a good faith belief that use of the material in the manner complained of is not authorized by the copyright owner, the owner's agent, or the law;
6. A statement that the information in the notification is accurate, and, under the pains and penalties of perjury, that you are authorized to act on behalf of the copyright owner.

*What are the consequences for someone at the university who has illegally downloaded and shared copyrighted material?* Each university can handle the disciplinary action in whatever way is best for them. Some universities will take this opportunity as a teachable moment to instruct primarily students in the right way to use copyrighted works. If the infringements continue, then students can have their access to university networks suspended indefinitely and in extreme cases be expelled from the university. If it is a university employee that has allegedly infringed, then various disciplinary actions can be taken and even termination can occur for repeated violations. These are all internal measures that are generally spelled out as conditions of employment or enrollment at the university.

However, even if the infringing material is taken down or removed from the network, the copyright owner can still pursue legal action. One of the first steps is to ask the courts to subpoena the records from the university that identifies the person associated with the IP address. Universities are required to release that information if the subpoena is legally accurate. Once the copyright owner has the name of the alleged infringer, then they can sue them for copyright infringement or settle with them out of court for a specific sum of money. The Recording Industry Association of America (RIAA) is a trade group that represents many of the major record labels and is notorious for pursuing legal action against college students and other alleged infringers.[4]

*What happens if the DMCA notice is in error?* There can certainly be times when a DMCA takedown notice inaccurately identifies a work or an IP address. If after an investigation the ISP can determine that there was an error after the material has been taken down, then under the DMCA procedures, they can then repost it. Recently, Elsevier, a major publisher of academic journals, sent a wave of takedown notices to universities to remove articles from university websites.[5] The articles were written by the university faculty but Elsevier claimed copyright. In such cases, the faculty would need to check their publication agreement with Elsevier to determine if they retained any rights. There are some agreements that allow faculty to post the author's final version on their website but not the published version or the version of record. If the author did retain the right, then Elsevier did not have a valid claim and the work could be reposted.

## Production Services

Many universities have departments that are responsible for marketing the university: for providing videotaping services for classes and university events; and for offering assistance to faculty, staff, students, and others with media issues. Each of these areas encounters copyright questions.

Marketing departments within universities use images, videotapes, interviews, and so on to showcase the strengths and uniqueness of the university. Unless the works are public domain materials, for example, photographs of the school when it was founded in the mid-1800s, then the works are protected by copyright. Many marketing departments generate their own works and so the copyright is undoubtedly owned by the university due to work-for-hire agreements. However, if images are used that are not created by university employees, then there should be an analysis of the copyright issues. Who owns the copyright? Do any exceptions apply such as fair use? More than likely, given the potentially broad use of the works, permission from the copyright owner would be required.

Videotaping services can include videotaping class lectures, guest speakers, job candidates, and a host of other scenarios. The videographer is usually employed by the university, so the copyright in the video would be owned by the university unless there was an agreement to the contrary.

But issues arise in who and what is being videotaped and how that videotape will be used. For example, the university has invited a famous photojournalist to speak to the campus. They bring with them a montage of their work that is displayed as they speak. Or a candidate for position at the university is required to give a presentation to their potential colleagues. They use a PowerPoint presentation that they developed that includes not only their own copyrighted work, but images, videos, and music where the copyright resides in a third party. Or a professor has the class videotaped so it can be used in another venue. Where the presentations were not videotaped the fair-use exception would more than likely apply. However, videotaping could potentially alter the copyright status.

Extemporaneous speeches are not protected under copyright because they do not meet the requirement that the work must be fixed. When the speech is videotaped, it is then fixed and protected under the law. Questions arise as to what rights the speaker might have in that videotape? Did the speaker sign an agreement with the university that allowed the videotaping of the session and detailed the copyright ownership of the work? Did the agreement address the issue of any third-party content included in the presentation? The copyrighted works that the speaker used as part of the presentation might have been fair use, but with the additional layer of the videotape, the speaker might need permission from the copyright owner to include the works.

Another issue that needs to be resolved prior to the videotaping is how the videotape will be used. Will it be hosted on a site that is restricted to only a small group of people, or will it be posted on the university website for anyone to view? Answers to these questions will determine what rights are needed by the university.

A professor that has his or her class videotaped must be aware of what rights the students have in that type of situation. If they can be identified, then there could potentially be a violation of their right of privacy. Before any such videotaping takes place, the professor should be aware of university policies regarding class videotaping as well as whether or not students need to agree to be videotaped. In such an instance, release forms signed by the students and detailing what they are agreeing to might need to be implemented. There can be potential liability issues if the policy is not followed.

## Media Services

Many universities provide media services to their faculty and staff. Services can range from converting VHS tapes to DVDs or vinyl albums to CDs to digitizing photographs. The conversion of VHS tapes to DVDs is generally one of the most frequent requests received by media services departments. Some of the questions that the department should ask the client before agreeing to any conversion include:

1. Is the content of the VHS tape available in a DVD format? If it is, then the DVD should be purchased by the client. There is no apparent

exception under the copyright law that would allow for the conversion by the media services department. Permission would be needed from the copyright holder for the conversion. The individual might be able to convert it him- or herself for personal use, but having a third party such as a media services department do the conversion takes the copyright analysis in a different direction. There could be legal implications for the university if there is an infringement, since the staff in the media department are employees of the university.

2. If the content is not available in a DVD format, then basic questions need to be asked such as whether the work is protected by copyright. If it is a U.S. federal government work or published in the United States prior to 1923, then it is public domain and can be converted without further investigation or analysis.

3. If it is protected, then what is the purpose of the conversion? Is it for classroom use, personal use, or to sell copies of it? Is it a preservation copy for the library? If it is for the library, then more than likely the libraries exception, section 108, would apply and it would be fine to make the conversion, although, of course, the digital copy would be subject to the section 108 restrictions. If it is for classroom use, then a VCR should be used to play the VHS tape. Unfortunately, this is where educators find themselves between a rock and a hard place. Many schools have removed VCRs from the classroom and either installed DVD players or now rely on a server to stream the media. So even though VCRs are available in the marketplace they are not available in the classroom. At this point, media departments must make a decision as to whether to rely on fair use and assume liability if they should guess incorrectly or have a policy that all such instances would require permission from the copyright holder before any conversion takes place. However, if the VHS tape is going to be used for distance education, then the conversion is allowed but only for reasonable and limited portions as defined by section 110(2) of the U.S. Copyright Act known as the TEACH Act.

4. What are the options if permissions are unavailable? If the copyright holder of the VHS tape is not one of the major motion picture studios, then many times the business has been purchased by another company or gone out of business with no contact information. If after investigation there is no concrete information as to the whereabouts of the copyright holder, then the media department again has to make a difficult choice as to whether or not to rely on fair use and take the risk that the copyright holder does not appear at a later time demanding compensation or just refuse to make the conversion due to the potential liability. This is a classic orphan work scenario.

Another major conversion issue for media departments revolves around region codes on DVDs. Region codes restrict the playing of the DVD to a certain region of the world. In this way the copyright holder can restrict the viewing of the DVD to only certain areas. For example, a DVD that is purchased in Italy or Europe might not play on a DVD player in the United States or North America. It is not unusual for faculty who teach and research in other countries to purchase DVDs for their courses in those countries and then want to use them in their home country but are then surprised when they return home to find that the DVD does not work in their player. There are multi-regional players that can be purchased, which would solve the problem. However if that is not an option, then in order to circumvent the technology, permission is needed or the department can rely on fair use after applying a risk analysis.

## Alumni Services/Advancement Offices

The digitization of yearbooks and student newspapers and posting them to institutional websites has been trending in recent years. Some archives and special collections departments in libraries are taking on the enormous task while other universities and K–12 schools are parceling it out to various departments, many times as part of an alumni association project, or even outsourcing it. If the libraries move forward with the digitization, then they have the additional protection of the libraries exception, section 108, subject to the circulation restrictions of digital copies. Digitization by other departments would have to rely on only the fair use exception. Before one contemplates digitizing yearbooks, they should consider the following questions:

1. Is the yearbook protected by copyright? Many yearbooks could potentially be in the public domain. There are several ways that the work could be public domain. If it was published prior to 1923, then it is in the public domain. If it was published prior to 1978 and did not have a copyright notice, then it is in the public domain. If it did have a copyright notice but the copyright was not renewed according to the copyright requirements, then the yearbook is in the public domain.

2. If the yearbook is protected, then who owns the copyright to it? If the work was published prior to 1978, then a copyright notice is required on it that indicates who owns the copyright. However, from 1978 until the current time, no notice is required. Most often the school will retain copyright, but if there is no statement of ownership, then one must conduct an investigation. There are multiple copyrighted works in a yearbook. Did a professional photographer take the individual

photos of the students? If so, did the photographer retain the copyright? If so, is the person even in business any longer? Did the school sign an agreement with the photographer delineating the rights? If so, is there a copy of the agreement available to review? Sometimes, there is a yearbook committee with student photographers who snap candid pictures of the seniors. Who owns the copyright in those pictures—the student or the school? Is there a school policy that defines copyright ownership of works created while the student is enrolled in the school? In some schools, seniors are allowed to customize their page. This could involve adding pictures of family or friends, poems, lyrics from songs, and so on. Just on one page there could be multiple copyrights. Did the student provide the school with permissions from the copyright holders? It is highly unlikely.

3. What are the options if determining copyright ownership is inconclusive? If after a reasonable investigation, copyright ownership cannot be determined, then the school must do a risk assessment. There is generally a low risk associated with digitizing yearbooks, but there is still some risk involved. Some institutions do not want to incur any risk. If that is the situation, then the yearbooks will remain in print only.

Identifying copyright holders for student newspapers can be easier than for yearbooks. Most university student newspapers are a legal entity in and of themselves and are independent of the university. They are generally incorporated bodies with the corporation comprised of past student writers/employees. Student writers are considered employees of the corporation and so under the work-for-hire doctrine, the copyright in the works they produce for the newspaper would reside with the employer. The copyright in the newspaper and the articles contained therein would be held by the corporation, so seeking permission to digitize them should not be an arduous task.

Advancement offices, which can also be known as development offices, are charged with raising funds to support university initiatives. Some of the issues involving deeds of gift to libraries were covered in an earlier chapter. However, there are many other gifts of copyrighted works that are received by the university and outside the purview of the library. It is important for the advancement offices to have a clear understanding of the copyright issues involved in any gift of intellectual property when crafting agreements with donors. Other gifts to the university could also include rights of publicity for famous alumni, and imbedded in that right can be copyright terms that can impact the use of the alumni's persona.

## Disability Service Centers

Students who are visually or hearing impaired can face challenges in reading and hearing the assignments for their classes. Sometimes a book needs to be read to the student by a machine or translated into Braille, while a video might need to be captioned for the hearing impaired. All of these works are more than likely protected by copyright and any changes or additions to them could be considered derivative works requiring permission from the copyright holder.

Disabilities services offices on campuses are charged with making an accommodation to students with disabilities so that they can have opportunity for education equal to students without disabilities. The Copyright Act has somewhat addressed this issue with the addition of what is known as the Chafee Amendment.[6] Congress added this provision in 1996 to allow certain types of organizations to provide accessible versions of published, nondramatic literary copyrighted works to blind or other persons with disabilities. Nonprofit educational institutions would qualify as one of the organizations under Chafee.

The World Intellectual Property Organization (WIPO) has recently addressed the issue of providing access to printed works for the blind and visually impaired. On June 28, 2013, WIPO adopted the "Marrakesh Treaty to Facilitate Access to Published Works for Persons Who Are Blind, Visually Impaired, or Otherwise Print Disabled."[7] The treaty requires countries to include an exception in their copyright laws that would allow for printed works to be made into accessible formats for people with print disabilities. The United States is already in compliance with the treaty because of the Chafee Amendment but it opens up cross-border trade with other countries who will now have a similar exception.

In addition to the Chafee Amendment, Congress passed and President George H. W. Bush signed into law in 1990 the Americans with Disabilities Act (ADA),[8] which guarantees people with disabilities the same opportunities as anyone else. Accommodations for education are part of the ADA.

Disability services offices must have an understanding and working knowledge of both the U.S. Copyright Act and the ADA in order to provide the necessary services to students. If a copyrighted work has already been converted into an accessible format that meets the needs of the student, then the department should opt to use that converted work. However, for example there are times where there might not be captioning available for a video that the student needs to view. The department has access to captioning technology and will use that to make the format accessible for the student. A word of caution is needed though. There are companies who offer captioning services.

Anyone who avails themselves of the service must agree to the terms of use. The terms can include a section whereby the user warrants that they have the rights to authorize the captioning. There is also generally some language about having permission of the copyright holder. Any agreements must be carefully read and understood before signing up for the service.

In addition to purchasing the work in the format that is needed, departments can also apply fair use or seek permission from the copyright holder if that is a better fit with their policies. The Chafee Amendment and the ADA provide quite a bit of latitude to staff who need to provide disability resources to students.

## Financial Aid Services

Copyright issues are found in financial aid offices as well due to provisions in the Higher Education Opportunity Act of 2008 (HEOA).[9] The act has copyright requirements that copyright officers and IT staff need to be familiar with in order to be in compliance.[10] The provisions were included in the act to limit illegal peer-to-peer (P2P) file sharing on university networks.

Universities must inform students that distribution of copyrighted materials without the copyright holder's permission or subject to one of the exceptions is an infringement of copyright. Such infringements have civil and criminal penalties associated with them, which the students are required to be aware of as well. The institution must also describe their own policies on illegal downloading and any penalties associated with that. Universities must provide alternatives to illegal downloading. Educause has an excellent website that updates the alternatives universities can link to in order to satisfy one prong of HEOA.[11]

Most of the HEOA requirements for providing information and discouraging illegal downloading were already being addressed at many universities. However, the new regulations do require that the universities' plans be documented and subject to review by the U.S. Department of Education. HEOA only applies to schools that want to receive federal student financial aid from the Department of Education.

## Continuing Education Services

Administrators at universities are grappling with the new phenomenon in higher education called massive open online courses, or MOOCs for short. "In 2012, 26 percent of academic leaders disagreed that MOOC's were 'a sustainable method for offering courses.' In 2013 that number leapt to 39 percent."[12] However, universities are still investigating offering MOOCs. The 2013 Babson survey found that 5 percent of institutions were actually offering MOOCs but 9 percent more had MOOCs planned for their campuses.[13] There is no charge for the courses and they are available to anyone who has access to a computer. They are not taken for credit toward a degree at the institution that is offering them and there are no admission requirements. Courses are generally taught by faculty at the institution and include a syllabus, readings, and class assignments similar to traditional courses. These are distinctly different from online programs offered at universities for credit where there is usually a fee.

MOOCs have generated lots of discussions on copyright.[14] The following are some of the most common questions and concerns.

1. Who owns the copyright to the course? Most institutions allow their faculty to own the copyright to the materials they create for a course such as the syllabus, assignments, PowerPoint presentations, class notes, and so on. However, MOOCs can be a game changer in how universities approach faculty copyright ownership of courses. Universities can contribute quite a bit in terms of infrastructure to support MOOCs. They will have to tackle the issue of whether or not such increased support as compared to the current traditional instruction models alters the copyright ownership. What also must be taken into consideration is that there are commercial providers of platforms for MOOCs who can potentially claim copyright ownership under terms of the contract with the institution.

2. What are the students rights regarding copyright? There are MOOCs where students play an active role in the course. They can write papers, submit assignments, participate in online chat sessions, and so on. Students generally retain their copyright in works they create as part of their education at a university. Will that remain the same policy in a MOOC? Should the university enter into an agreement with a third party to provide MOOC services, they must take into consideration student copyright issues. Is there language in the contract that assigns a nonexclusive license to the MOOC provider and/or the university to student works? What is the responsibility, if any, of the university to protect student intellectual property rights or to actively inform the students that their work could potentially be used in any way by the MOOC platform provider?

3. What copyright exceptions would faculty be able to utilize in a MOOC environment? They would not be able to use section 110(1) of the U.S. Copyright Act, since that only applies to the F2F classroom setting. The TEACH Act, which is section 110(2), allows for the digital transmission of certain types of works subject to a multitude of requirements. Most universities that are engaging in MOOCs are accredited

nonprofit educational institutions, which is a requirement of TEACH. Another requirement is that the transmission is restricted to only those students who are enrolled in the course. This begs the question, then, of does it matter if the class has 30 or 30,000 students in it? The one sticky requirement that might derail the TEACH option is that the class session must be offered as a regular part of the systematic mediated instructional activities. Would MOOCs qualify under that? It would certainly depend on how the university structured their MOOCs. The only remaining exception is fair use. This has probably the most possibilities. Faculty would have to carefully apply the fair-use analysis with an awareness of the open nature of the course and how that might impact the market effect factor. Fair use is definitely an option, but both faculty and universities might not want to assume the risk and instead opt to request permission and/or pay licensing fees to use the works.

MOOCs are still very much in an experimental phase. However, should universities move forward with this new educational model, then it would be in their best interest to address the copyright concerns prior to entering into the MOOC market.

**Provost Office**

Open access has been discussed in previous chapters as it relates to faculty and libraries. However, administrators ranging from provosts to policy groups are involved in the decision-making process of whether or not to formally promote open access on their campus. If the administration is considering spearheading a campaign to develop an open-access policy, then the following questions should be considered:

1. Is the policy developed by the faculty or the administration? Many times an open-access policy is more successful if there is a groundswell of support from the faculty and they take the initiative to draft the policy. Faculty are much more likely to embrace a policy that they have had input in developing rather than one mandated from the administration especially when it concerns their intellectual property rights.
2. What does the policy require of faculty? Most open-access policies require faculty to deposit the final author's manuscript of articles published in peer-reviewed journals to the institutional repository. Some publishers allow faculty to post the author's final peer-reviewed version but not the published version. Faculty need to play close attention to the language in the publishing contract. The open-access mandate generally does not include books, book chapters, conference proceedings, and

such, but faculty are encouraged to deposit those as well if they have retained the right to do so. Some policies will allow an embargo period of six to twelve months before the work is deposited into the repository. There can be opt-out provisions in policies that grant faculty permission to bypass the deposit process due to concerns for promotion and tenure.

3. How is copyright addressed in open-access policies? The copyright issue is one of the major stumbling blocks in open-access policies. One strategy is that universities retain a nonexclusive license to copyrightable works, specifically peer-reviewed journal articles, produced by faculty. The nonexclusive license allows the university to then populate the institutional repository with faculty intellectual output. Faculty would still retain copyright but subject to the grant to the university of the nonexclusive license. This can pose problems when faculty sign agreements with publishers transferring their copyright to the publisher. They must put the publisher on notice that the transfer has conditions based on the rights already granted to the university.

Each university drafts its own open-access policy to comply with the regulations that are in place at the institution as well as taking into account the university culture. However, many open-access policies model the Harvard policy[15] as their starting point and guide.

## Extension Services

The Morrill Act of 1862 established land-grant colleges and universities in every state by providing them with federal lands.[16] The mission of these institutions was to teach agriculture, military tactics, and the mechanic arts, which would provide a practical education. There has been additional federal legislation that builds upon the first Morrill Act to include historically black colleges and universities as well as Native American tribal colleges. To date, there are seventy-four land-grant colleges and universities that continue to "fulfill their mandate for openness, accessibility, and service to people through a variety of programs and activities."[17] They are not all public universities but include such private institutions as Cornell University and the Massachusetts Institute of Technology.[18] Such universities, particularly with agricultural schools, have extension services departments, which are responsible for disseminating university research including agricultural information to the citizens of their state generally through county extension offices. There are numerous copyright issues that arise in the course of conducting extension business particularly due to the conflict between the missions of land-grant colleges and universities and the U.S. Copyright Act. Below are some typical questions.

1. Who owns the copyright to extension publications? Extension offices usually publish and distribute a large number of items. The question of who owns the copyright to the publications can be difficult to determine at times, particularly for older publications. The first question that needs to be asked is if the author is an employee of the university. If the answer is affirmative, then the next question is what the author's employee classification is. If the author is a faculty member and the institution allows faculty to retain their copyright, then the author would own the copyright in the publication. However, if the author is a staff member, then the copyright in the work would be owned by the university. It appears pretty straightforward, but there can be complications.

   Sometimes extension employees can be assigned to the university but actually be employed by the state or the U.S. Department of Agriculture, or sometimes a position is split between the university and a state or federal government agency. If the author is a federal employee, then there is no copyright that would attach to the publication, but any other designation would have copyright ownership. There can also be occasions where the publication is a result of a grant. If this is the case, then one must look to the grant documentation to determine who owns the copyright for any works produced as a result of the grant. It is in the best interest of all concerned to establish copyright ownership prior to the creation of a work.

2. How can I legally distribute works published by other state extension services? It is not uncommon for state extension services to post or republish other extension services works. For example, an extension service in Louisiana might have numerous publications that are useful to other states, such as how to eradicate mold from houses after a flood. After severe flooding, another state may want to distribute the Louisiana information to its citizens. If the work is not a federal government document but does have a copyright attached to it, then the copyright law would apply, and one must look at the available exceptions such as fair use. However, even though extension services technically own the copyright, they are known to work together and share information, which is the intent of the Morrill Act. Many times there will be general permissions posted on extension websites, which allow users to republish and distribute the information.

3. A county extension office publishes a newsletter and would like to include recipes in it. Are recipes protected by copyright? Recipes can have copyright protection if there is any type of literary description accompanying it. The listing of ingredients would not be protected, but the story behind it would be, and any illustrations would be as well.

There are various and numerous complex copyright issues that extension services must confront and address. It can be confusing attempting to determine copyright ownership and use issues when there can be apparent conflicts between university policies and the law. A clear-cut understanding of the issues will facilitate the advancement of the extension services mission.

## UNIVERSITY-OWNED COPYRIGHTS

### Technology Transfer

Universities own numerous copyrights ranging from images to software to texts to videos. The management of copyrights is usually handled by a technology transfer or commercialization office. Copyrights are generally considered the poor cousin to patents since patents generate more revenue for an institution. However, copyrights can be a valuable asset if managed correctly. Due to the large number of copyrights generated on a daily basis at universities, it is difficult if not impossible to keep accurate records of them. Some universities require employees whose work product is owned by the university to self-disclose any copyrightable work that they produce that might have value in the marketplace. This is one way of compiling an inventory of university-owned copyrighted works that could potentially generate revenue.

Permissions from external sources to use university-owned copyrighted works are received daily. They are generally funneled through the technology transfer office. Sometimes it is difficult to ascertain if the university truly does own the copyright in a work if detailed records have not been kept over the years. Employees might no longer be associated with the university. A work could be a joint effort between a faculty member and someone who is a staff member, which can thereby muddle the question of copyright ownership. In such cases where the university is unable to definitively prove ownership, it might grant permission but with the caveat that it can only provide permission to the rights that it might have in the work.

### University Presses

University presses can sometimes be a distinct legal entity from an institution or they can be a part of it. Either way, there is some association with the university and there are always copyright issues embedded in any publishing endeavor. If the press is a legal part of the university, then the university owns the copyright to the works unless there is an agreement with the author to the contrary. As open access becomes more recognized as an acceptable option to the traditional publishing model and with the increase of open-access policies at institutions, university presses are developing contracts that are more author friendly. Such contracts allow the author to retain the copyright but gives the press the exclusive right to be the first to publish the work.

In addition to the copyright ownership issue, university presses have decisions to make regarding fair use and permissions. With traditional commercial publishers, authors must provide the publisher with permissions for any third-party content included in the author's work. The expense for obtaining such permissions is typically borne by the author. Many times such third-party content could be fair use, but publishers do not want to risk any liability, which is why they require the permissions. University presses have leeway in how they choose to handle the same issues. Being a part of a university, they are front and center in scholarly communication debates and well versed in how critical fair use is in the educational environment. University presses might be willing to assume the risk and allow for fair use when appropriate in order to further their university's mission.

In recent years some university presses have been incorporated into libraries. They offer not only traditional works by a university press but also have taken on the role of library publishing services, which includes the institutional repository. A report funded by a National Leadership Grant from the U.S. Institute of Museum and Library Services found that partnerships between libraries and presses is becoming more frequent on campuses as budgets decline and missions begin to merge.[19] The alliances provide benefits to all. Responses to copyright inquiries can have one voice that represents the whole rather than bifurcated approaches.

## CONCLUSION

The scope of copyright issues addressed by a copyright officer for staff and administrators is quite broad. Copyright education must reach all levels of a university, since copyright impacts so many diverse areas. It is also important for the copyright officer to be aware of not only the U.S. Copyright Act but any other law that has copyright implications, such as HEOA, in order to assist staff in complying with the law.

## NOTES

1. Dwayne K. Buttler, "Music and Copyright," in *Copyright Law for Librarians and Educators: Creative Strategies and Practical Solutions*, ed. Kenneth D. Crews (Chicago: American Library Association, 2012), 112.

2. Buttler, "Music and Copyright," 113.

3. U.S. Copyright Act, 17 U.S.C. § 1201.

4. Electronic Frontier Foundation, "RIAA v. The People: Five Years Later," September 30, 2008, accessed April 10, 2014, https://www.eff.org/wp/riaa-v-people -five-years-later.

5. Andrea Peterson, "How One Publisher Is Stopping Academics from Sharing Their Research," *Washington Post*, December 19, 2013, accessed April 10, 2014, http://www.washingtonpost.com/blogs/the-switch/wp/2013/12/19/how-one -publisher-is-stopping-academics-from-sharing-their-research/.

6. U.S. Copyright Act, 17 U.S.C. § 121.

7. World Intellectual Property Organization, "Marrakesh Treaty to Facilitate Access to Published Works for Persons Who Are Blind, Visually Impaired, or Otherwise Print Disabled," 2013, accessed April 10, 2014, http://www.wipo.int/meetings/en/ doc_details.jsp?doc_id=245323.

8. Americans with Disabilities Act of 1990, Public Law 101-336, U.S. Statutes at Large 104 Stat. 327 (1990), codified at 42 U.S.C. 12101 et seq.

9. Higher Education Opportunity Act of 2008, Pub. L. 110-315, 122 Stat. 3078 (2008), 20 U.S.C. § 1001 et seq.

10. Educause, "7 Things You Should Know about the P2P Provisions of the HEOA," 2010, accessed April 9, 2014, http://www.educause.edu/library/resources/ 7-things-you-should-know-about-p2p-provisions-heoa.

11. Educause, "Legal Sources of Online Content," 2013, accessed April 10, 2014, http://www.educause.edu/focus-areas-and-initiatives/policy-and-security/educause -policy/issues-and-positions/intellectual-property/legal-sources-onli.

12. Steve Kolowich. "Doubts about MOOC's Continue to Rise, Survey Finds." *Chronicle of Higher Education*, January 15, 2014, accessed April 10, 2014, https:// chronicle.com/article/Doubts-About-MOOCs-Continue-to/144007/.

13. I. Elaine Allen and Jeff Seaman, *Grade Change: Tracking Online Education in the United States* (Waltham, MA: Babson Survey Research Group, 2014), accessed April 10, 2014, http://www.onlinelearningsurvey.com/reports/gradechange.pdf.

14. Educause, "Copyright Challenges in a MOOC Environment," 2013 accessed April 9, 2014, http://www.educause.edu/library/resources/copyright-challenges -mooc-environment.

15. Stuart M. Shieber, *A Model Open-Access Policy, Version 1.11* (Cambridge, MA: Harvard University, 2013), accessed April 10, 2014, https://osc.hul.harvard.edu/ sites/default/files/model-policy-annotated_01_2013.pdf.

16. Morrill Act, Pub. L. 37-108 (1862); 7 U.S.C. § 301 et seq.

17. Association of Public and Land-Grant Universities, "About Us," 2013, accessed April 9, 2014, http://www.aplu.org/page.aspx?pid=1565.

18. Association of Public and Land-Grant Universities, "About Us."

19. J. L. Mullins, C. Murray-Rust, J. L. Ogburn, R. Crow, O. Ivins, A. Mower, D. Nesdill, M. P. Newton, J. Speer, and C. Watkinson, *Library Publishing Services: Strategies for Success: Final Research Report* (Washington, DC: SPARC, 2012).

# 9

## Copyright Services for Students

Students at both the undergraduate and graduate level are confronted with copyright issues on a daily basis. Some understand that and others do not until they are faced with a situation such as a notice of copyright infringement. In some respects the issues are a bit different for graduate students, who are looking at how their publications will enhance their career opportunities. Undergraduates tend to focus more on the assignments at hand and passing the course. Over the years, I have seen more interest by faculty in helping educate the students on copyright, particularly for students who major in the visual and performing arts.

### THESES AND DISSERTATIONS

Doctoral students in most disciplines must complete a dissertation as part of the graduation requirements. Depending upon their major some master's students must complete a thesis as part of their program. Many years of research and writing go into the final product. More often than not the copyright issues are not addressed until deadlines are near. Many universities require that graduate students submit their dissertation or thesis to the vendor ProQuest, which publishes a database of graduate students' works, although some universities are beginning to give students options as to where to publish their dissertation.[1] Copyright issues for dissertations and theses generally revolve around third-party content that is included in them. ProQuest requires students to attach written permissions for any third-party content included in the dissertation or thesis. It could be an image, a chart, graph, or such. If permission is not included, then ProQuest will block that portion of the dissertation.

Obtaining permissions can be a long and daunting process if good records are not kept of the sources used. For example, an art history major might have used dozens of images from the web but neglected to adequately retain the web addresses where the images were found. Trying to recreate the search to obtain the same results can sometimes be impossible. Websites or images on them disappear. They might find a similar image but maybe not the exact one that they had originally planned to use. It can be very time consuming, since the student is then basically starting from the beginning. Once the source has been obtained the student needs to contact the copyright holder, not necessarily the website that posted the image, since that site might not be the owner of the copyright. If the student is able to identify the copyright owner, he or she might still not be able to locate that party. In such a case, the student needs to decide whether to substitute something similar or just not use any image. If the correct owner is located, then the student must be very careful in wording the request for permission to use. Chapters of dissertations can sometimes be turned into articles, or the dissertation as a whole may be published as a book, so the student would be wise to request the broadest permission possible so as not to have to keep returning to the copyright owner for future requests.

A recent trend with dissertations is where students enter into an agreement with a publisher and have chapters of their dissertation published as articles prior to the submission of the dissertation to their university. They then need to reproduce the article in its entirety to be included as one of their dissertation chapters. This can pose a problem if they did not retain the copyright. If they transferred the copyright to the publisher in exchange for the article being published, then they need to obtain permission from the publisher to include the work in their dissertation. However, there are some publishers who have language in their agreements that allow authors to include their article in their dissertation. The student needs to read the agreement quite closely to make sure that the language is incorporated into the contract before they sign it. If it is not included, then they should negotiate the changes so they do not find themselves in the position of having to rewrite a dissertation chapter should the publisher not give them permission to reproduce the article.

Fair use more than likely can apply in many situations where third-party content is included, such as with a quote or with an entire image. A recent 2013 case highlighted the application of fair use to quotes.[2] William Faulkner's estate sued Sony Pictures for copyright infringement for a line used in the Woody Allen movie *Midnight in Paris*. One of the actors in the film says, "The past is not dead. It's not even past," which was taken from Faulkner's *Requiem for a Nun* where he wrote "The past is never dead. It's not even past."[3] The judge found in favor of Sony Pictures. He did a fair-use analysis and determined that Sony's use of Faulkner's quote was fair use and that the use was de minimis. Short quotes similar to ones in the Sony case appear to be more acceptable to some publishers, generally university presses, but not entire works, such as an image. However, most major publishers including ProQuest are risk averse so even if fair use is applicable it is not generally an option.

Below are some of the most asked questions from a graduate student to a copyright officer.

*Who owns the copyright to my dissertation/thesis?* The answer to this question has multiple levels. Students must check university policies to determine the answer. Copyright in works produced as part of their education usually belong to the students. Some universities can claim a nonexclusive license in the works for promotional and pedagogical purposes but not for commercial purposes. This would allow the university to post student works such as art, videos, and so on. On their website to showcase the talent of their student body. Copyright will then reside with the student until it is transferred to someone else, which can occur should the student enter into a contract with a publisher or other content holder.

*Is my dissertation/thesis considered published when it is deposited to ProQuest?* Under the U.S. Copyright Act,[4] "Publication is the distribution of copies or phonorecords of a work to the public by sale or other transfer of ownership, or by rental, lease, or lending. The offering to distribute copies of phonorecords to a group of persons for purposes of further distribution, public performance, or public display, constitutes publication."

In such a case, the copyright law recognizes it as a publication, but many disciplines do not. It is well understood in most fields that students are required by their universities to submit their dissertation/thesis to ProQuest as a condition of graduation. Publishers who require that any work submitted to them for publication not be previously published generally do not recognize the dissertation in ProQuest as a publication.

*I have been working with my professor on a research project and the professor has just published a paper I wrote analyzing the research data but did not include my name on it. The professor claims that I work for him and that the intellectual property rights in my research belong to him. Is that correct?* One of the key questions in analyzing this situation is what is meant by the phrase "work for him." Is this a work-for-hire scenario whereby the professor hired the graduate student to work with him on the research project and has a contract stating the terms of employment including intellectual property rights? If so, and the contract is specific on the issues, then the professor could indeed own the copyright to the paper. However, what if the scenario is changed slightly and the graduate student has been hired by the university to assist with the professor's research? If that is the case then potentially it could be the university that holds the copyright to the paper and not the graduate student or the professor. Both would be employees of the university and their work product would be owned by the employer unless there is an agreement to the contrary. The more likely scenario, though, is that the graduate student is working with the professor as part of his or her course work or program and there is no employer-employee relationship. If the joint author requirements are met, such as that the intent was to create a joint work at the time the work was created, that the works would be merged into a whole, and that each author contributed a copyrightable work, then both the professor and the graduate student would own a copyright in the work. The bone of contention with this could be the intent requirement. There are some professors who assume that any work done by graduate students in their labs or under their supervision is then owned by them. It is in the best interest of all concerned if there is an understanding of the rights prior to the commencement of any work.

*I have heard that when multiple authors are listed on a journal article, that it is only the first author who has the copyright in the work. Is that true?* It may be that none of the authors own the copyright if they transferred the copyright to the publisher in order to have the work published. However, prior to transferring any rights, the order of the names does not dictate who owns the copyright in the work. When the article is a jointly authored work between a professor and graduate students, the professor's name might be the first name, based upon name recognition in the field. If it is truly a jointly authored work under the copyright law, then each author has a copyright in it.

*I have included figures, such as models, charts, and graphs, in my dissertation/thesis to demonstrate my research. I took these from various books and articles, since the figures are all well known and accepted in my field. Are they copyrighted? If so, can I make some minor changes to them and claim the copyright for myself?* There is a concept in copyright law called the merger doctrine, where the idea and the expression of the idea are not really distinguishable from each other. When the idea behind the expression can only be expressed in a limited number of ways, then it is more factual in nature and not protectable under the copyright law.[5]

There was a recent case in the Seventh Circuit Court of Appeals, *Ho v. Taflove*,[6] which involved disputes between two engineering professors and their grad students around a mathematical model. The court cited section 102(b) of the U.S. Copyright Act which states, "In no case does copyright protection for an original work of authorship extend to any idea, procedure, process, system, method of operation, concept, principle, or discovery, regardless of the form in which it is described, explained, illustrated, or embodied in such work." The Court determined that the mathematical model in dispute could only be described in a few ways and merged the idea with the expression.

The organization, chart colors, fonts, and so forth could be protected under copyright law but not the process.

## STUDENT USE OF COPYRIGHTED WORKS

Undergraduate students are using copyrighted works more than likely on a daily basis. In my experience most are not overly concerned about copyright and sharing copyrighted works since their peers are all doing it as well. They cannot understand the constraints imposed upon them under copyright and believe that the law is antiquated. I have found over the years that there are two events that capture their attention. The first is when their work is shared in a way that they do not like without their permission and the second is when they receive legal notice of alleged infringing activity. As part of an educational institution, these are considered teachable moments.

Students use copyrighted works for their courses and for personal use and sometimes they are the creators of copyrighted works. For the use side there is a continuum of how copyrighted works can be used in the classroom and beyond. Sometimes it can be a onetime use, while other times it is used repeatedly in a variety of different venues. The initial question to the student is: How are you going to use this work? Then the question morphs into whether they have any plans to use it beyond the initial use.

A common scenario is that a student needs to incorporate a copyrighted work into a class assignment. For example, it could be a series of images for a paper, video clips and music for a PowerPoint presentation, or a full video. The following are some of the queries that should be posed to students.

1. How are you going to use the work? Is it for a classroom assignment? If students use a copyrighted work for a course assignment that is restricted to just the classroom, even if it is a hybrid course, then the use would generally be fair use. If they are incorporating the work into a new work that they created, then there is an even stronger fair-use argument. To take it one step further, if they make changes to the work, such as repurposing it, then it could be categorized as a transformative work, which generates even more protection under the copyright law. When students analyze their use under the four fair-use factors, it can appear as follows:
   a. Purpose and character—purpose is for educational use and could be for criticism and commentary, which weighs in favor of fair use. The work could also be transformative, making a whole new work, which would also qualify as fair use under this factor.

    b. The nature of the work can be factual or creative. The student would
       have to look closely at that to make the determination.

    c. The amount of the work used could be 100 percent if it is an image,
       or it could be a minimal amount if it is only seconds of a song.

    d. There is probably no market effect on the original since the student
       is only showing it to a very limited audience. This factor would then
       weigh in favor of fair use.

2. Where did you get the work? It is important that the work that is being
   used is a lawfully made copy. If it is a pirated copy, then many of the
   exceptions will not be applicable. It's also a good lesson for the students
   to be aware of where they obtain material and to evaluate most often
   websites where they download it from.

3. What do you intend to do with the work once your assignment is completed? This can be a difficult question for some students to respond
   to initially. Their focus is on completing the assignment for the course
   and not necessarily looking to the future. However, what if it is a video
   that they created and they want to show it at a conference? What about
   entering it into a video contest? What about adding it to their portfolio
   to be distributed to potential employers? What about posting it on their
   website? This is the continuum that was referenced earlier where the
   work was intended for only one use but now the student wants to take it
   beyond the classroom. A fair-use analysis must be conducted for each
   use of the work. More than likely, it is fair use for the course assignment, but it might not be if they post it on their unrestricted website.

## STUDENTS AS OWNERS OF COPYRIGHTED WORKS

Students are also owners of copyrighted works and most of the time they do
not even realize that. They hold copyrights for probably thousands of works
ranging from papers to photographs to videos to e-mails. The following is a
sampling of typical questions posed by students.

1. How do I restrict others from using my copyrighted works? This time
   the shoe is on the other foot, and it's not always comfortable. Some find
   it perfectly fine to use other people's works but feel quite protective of
   their own works. The harsh reality is that once the work is made public,
   such as posting it to an unrestricted website, then others can use the
   works if they qualify for one of the exceptions under the copyright law.

2. I want to share my work with the world but retain some control. How
   do I do that? You can attach a Creative Commons license to your work.

Creative Commons is a nonprofit organization that was founded to provide people with a way to share their works under one of the licenses developed by Creative Commons. The premise behind Creative Commons is to create a community of users that could share their works and allow others to build upon them legally. They designed numerous nonexclusive licenses that can be attached to a work that allow others to use them either very broadly, narrowly, or somewhere in between. There are currently seven licenses that creators can choose from.[7]

a. CC-BY—This license is very flexible. The only requirement is that the original work be given attribution.

b. CC-BY-ND—Requires attribution and no changes can be made to the original, which in legal terms means no derivative works allowed. However, this license does allow both commercial and noncommercial use.

c. CC-BY-NC-SA—The work can be built upon but only for noncommercial use. The new work must be licensed under the same terms and must include attribution.

d. CC-BY-SA—This license allows the work to be built upon and can be used commercially. There must be attribution and it must be licensed under the same terms.

e. CC-BY-NC—The new work must include an attribution and can only be used for noncommercial purposes. However, this license allows the new work to be licensed any way the user wants.

f. CC-BY-NC-ND—This is the most restrictive of all the CC licenses. The works are only allowed to be shared and must include attribution. No changes can be made and they cannot use it commercially.

g. CC0—this license is the least restrictive of all. It, in essence, allows creators to waive all rights to their work.

3. How do mash-ups and remixes work with the copyright law? Remixes are used generally for music to create a new work by remixing a song. Mash-ups can be combinations of numerous works, mostly videos, to produce something new as well. The concept is certainly not new, but the technology allows for much more sophisticated works that can be distributed worldwide with the press of a button. Each work used in a remix or mash-up is probably protected by copyright unless the work is in the public domain. The only exception that would potentially apply would be fair use. The analysis would have to be applied to each use of the work and not just the new work as a whole. Are the changes or additions that are being made to the work, really substantive or are they minor? Do they really transform the work or is it basically the same? Is this a parody, such as the case of 2 Live Crew's rendition of "Oh,

Pretty Woman" discussed in an earlier chapter? Another question that should be asked is will the new work be a substitute for the original work, thereby harming the market? There is an incredibly clever mash-up video called "A Fair(y) Use Tale" created by Eric Faden of Bucknell University and distributed by The Media Education Foundation,[8] which uses Disney characters to explain copyright and fair use. Undoubtedly, Disney did not provide permission to use the clips in the video. However, it is an excellent example of a transformative work that mixes parody and commentary and would not compete in any way with the original full-length Disney cartoons.

4. I wanted to use a video that I found on YouTube for my project, but when I went back to download/link to it, the video had been removed. Why? Many people can upload videos to YouTube but that doesn't necessarily mean that they have the legal right to do so. If in YouTube's determination, the video is potentially infringing on someone's copyright, then they will take it down. Many times they will put a notice where the video had been posted indicating that there was a potential infringement.

5. I am an art student and part of the course is to draw live models. I posted my drawing of one of the models on Facebook only to have her contact me and demand that I remove it. I thought I owned the copyright. Am I legally required to remove it? As long as there is not a policy to the contrary, students own the copyrights in the works they create. A drawing as part of a class assignment would certainly fall into that category. If the students own the copyright, then they can do what they want with their work. The issue here might not be copyright but could be a contractual issue as well as a right of privacy issue. If the model signed a contract with the university prohibiting the use of her image except for the coursework, then there could be a breach of contract if the students also agreed to that. On the other hand, the contract with the model could allow for whatever purposes the students and the university choose. The bigger issue could be an invasion of privacy if the model did not consent to the use. Another issue to think about in this scenario is the work that was posted on Facebook. If the student did a drawing of the model in class, then he would have to take a picture of the drawing in order to post it to Facebook. If he took the photo, then the copyright in the photo would belong to him. However, if he did not or there were copyright ownership questions about the original drawing, then there could potentially be other copyright issues that would have to be addressed.

## STUDENTS AND SOCIAL MEDIA

Students use copyrighted works not only for educational purposes but for personal use as well. Social media sites are flourishing and are used extensively by students, whether it's Facebook, Twitter, Instagram, Snapchat, or Flickr, just to name a few. Such websites involve posting photographs or videos taken either by the person posting it or someone else. The media can be shared and reposted numerous times. One can only imagine the number of copyright infringements that take place on a daily basis.

Students can take a photo with their cell phone, post it on a social media site, and within seconds it can be seen around the world. Since they took the photo, then they would own the copyright in it. However, if the person who posts the photo was not the one that took the photo, then the posting could potentially be an infringement, and every time someone reposts it, there is another infringement. Copyright holders have the exclusive right to make copies of their work and distribute those copies subject to the exceptions under the copyright law. The only exception that would more than likely be applicable in this situation is fair use. After applying all four factors, the only one that might weigh in favor of fair use would be the fourth factor, which is market effect. Most photos are taken with family and friends, so unless it is a professional photographer, then there would be no real market for the photos. The copyright owners who do recognize and understand that an infringement has occurred generally choose not to enforce their copyright.

However, there was a 2013 case where a professional photographer, Daniel Morel, had posted his photos of the 2010 Haitian earthquake for sale on Twitter.[9] They were illegally copied by Lisandro Suero, who claimed they were his and sold them to the French agency, Agence France Presse (AFP), who in turn shared them as part of a license agreement with Getty Images in the United States. Most major networks along with newspapers used the images, some citing Suero as the photographer of several of the images and some citing Morel. Getty Images and AFP were both sued by Morel for copyright infringement. The court found in Morel's favor and awarded him $1.2 million.[10]

All participants in social media sites must agree to the company's terms of use before being allowed access to the site. There is usually a button where the user clicks "I Agree" to the terms whether or not they ever read them. The terms of use specifically state what rights the company has with the information posted on their site and what rights the user has. The terms can change at any time and it is up to users to keep track of the changes and understand what it means for them. Students agree to all the restrictions placed upon them through the social media sites never really understanding that they have just entered into a legally binding contract. Not only might they be subjecting themselves to claims of copyright infringement but also breach of contract.

## PLAGIARISM

An issue that students get confused about is the difference between copyright infringement and plagiarism. Students believe that if they cite their source then it does not matter how much of the work they use. Copyright infringement is when an illegal copy is made of a work or too much of a work is used without the benefit of one of the exceptions. Plagiarism is when a work is used and there is no attribution. They are two very different concepts with different penalties associated with them. Copyright is a federal law with a range of both civil and criminal penalties. There is no federal or state plagiarism law, but it is more of an ethical and moral issue. Fraud might be the end result of acts of plagiarism, but that is more of a long shot. Most universities have a student honor code that details what internal procedures the school will follow if a student is found guilty of plagiarism. The penalties can range from failing the course to expulsion from the university. Many famous people, such as historian authors Stephen Ambrose[11] and Doris Kearns Goodwin[12] and higher-education administrators have lost their jobs or had their career impacted when faced with allegations of plagiarism. So although there is no plagiarism law, the damage from it can quite substantial. Both plagiarism and copyright infringement can derail student careers.

## INTERNATIONAL STUDENTS

International students, primarily from China, India, and South Korea, make up a large part of many college campuses.[13] This poses challenges for both the students and the copyright officer. Copyright laws in other countries can be very different from U.S. law. Add the language barrier to that and it results in much misunderstanding and intervention. A common occurrence is the wholesale downloading of entire runs of journals by students who are graduating and returning to their native country. It is not only massive copyright infringement but generally a breach of contract since many times, university libraries have entered into license agreements with vendors for digital copies of the journals. Establishing an education program for international students on U.S. copyright law at the beginning of their matriculation to the university helps ease the tensions and sets them on the right track to success.

## CONCLUSION

Partnering with faculty and administrators to help educate the students on copyright is a good option in approaching the issue. There are penalties such as loss of computer privileges, which assists in getting their attention but the strategy also needs to take into account the longer term and the understanding of copyright that they will need once they leave the university. There are some students who will consistently break the law and thumb their nose at the rules and regulations. However, it has been my experience that most students want to use copyrighted works legally but sometimes just do not know how to do that. It is a great opportunity and benefits the student and the university to teach them the right way. Also, the other aspect that really captures their attention and interest is the discovery that they are copyright owners. Students become much more vested in understanding the copyright law when they have a stake in it.

## NOTES

1. Gail P. Clement, "American ETD Dissemination in the Age of Open Access," *C&RL News* 74 no. 11 (2013): 562–66.

2. Faulkner Literary Rights, LLC v. Sony Pictures Classics, Inc. 953 S. Supp. 2d 701 (N.D. Miss. July 18, 2013).

3. Eriq Gardner, "Sony Pictures Wins '*Midnight in Paris*' Lawsuit over Faulkner Quote (Exclusive)," *Hollywood Reporter*, July 18, 2013, accessed April 10, 2014, http://www.hollywoodreporter.com/thr-esq/sony-pictures-wins-midnight-paris-588515.

4. U.S. Copyright Act, 17 U.S.C. § 101.

5. Russell K. Hasan, "Winning the Copyright War: Copyright's Merger Doctrine and Natural Rights Theory as Solutions to the Problem of Reconciling Copyright and Free Speech," *Engage* 14 no. 1 (2013), accessed April 10, 2014, http://www.fed-soc.org/publications/detail/winning-the-copyright-war-copyrights-merger-doctrine-and-natural-rights-theory-as-solutions-to-the-problem-of-reconciling-copyright-and-free-speech.

6. Ho v. Taflove, 648 F.3d 489 (7th Cir. 2011).

7. Creative Commons, "Examples of Creative Commons License Use," accessed April 9, 2014, http://creativecommons.org/examples.

8. Eric Faden, 2007, "A Fair(y) Use Tale." *YouTube*, accessed April 9, 2014, http://www.youtube.com/watch?v=CJn_jC4FNDo.

9. Agence France Presse v. Daniel Morel v. Getty Images, et al., 934 F. Upp. 2d 547 (S.D.N.Y. January 14, 2013).

10. James Kosur, "Daniel Morel's Twitter Photos Sold without Permission, $1.2 Million Awarded," *Social News Daily*, November 22, 2013, accessed April 9, 2014,

http://socialnewsdaily.com/19909/daniel-morels-twitter-photos-sold-without-permis
sion-1-2-million-awarded/.

11. Mark Lewis, "Ambrose Problems Date Back to Ph.D. Thesis," *Forbes*, May
10, 2002, accessed April 10, 2014, http://www.forbes.com/2002/05/10/0510ambrose
.html.

12. David D. Kirkpatrick, "Historian's Fight for Her Reputation May Be Damaging It," *New York Times*, March 31, 2002, accessed April 10, 2014, http://www
.nytimes.com/2002/03/31/us/historian-s-fight-for-her-reputation-may-be-damaging
-it.html.

13. Bill Chappell, "Record Number of International Students Attend U.S. Colleges," *NPR*, November 11, 2013, accessed April 10, 2014, http://www.npr.org/blogs/
thetwo-way/2013/11/11/244601986/record-number-of-international-students-attend
-u-s-colleges.

# 10

# Next Steps and Future Considerations

Copyright is a very dynamic area of law. The Copyright Act does not get amended all that often, so copyright officers must look to the courts for interpretation of the various provisions within the law. They can also be guided in their decision-making process by discussions with colleagues, awareness of best practices that have been developed by various groups and associations, and keeping track of what's trending in the copyright environment.

There are some hot areas and recent developments that have the potential for shifting the balance of copyright. As indicated in previous chapters of this book, there is discussion on totally revamping the current copyright law. In addition there are provisions in the current law that have recently begun to impact major content industries such as movies, music, and publishers. They are known as the termination clauses. Also noteworthy are the best practices documents being issued by professional associations whose members are major users of copyrighted works.

However, although all of the speculation and armchair quarterbacking on how the courts will rule in certain cases and what a new copyright law might look like are exciting to ponder, the copyright officer has to deal with the issues that are presented on a daily basis. A copyright analysis, which applies the current law as well as relevant jurisdictional court cases, is the foundation that all copyright officers must build upon for successful outcomes.

## COPYRIGHT ANALYSIS

As seen in previous chapters, it is important to ask very specific questions when approached with a copyright issue in order to respond with good advice.

Examples of different scenarios and resulting questions have been expounded upon in earlier sections of this book. However, as a final reminder, conducting a general copyright analysis is the best way to begin and then the analysis should be followed up with fact-specific questions. The following is one way to conduct such a general analysis.

1. Ascertain if it is a copyright issue that is being posed. Many times the issue can be a contract one or a trademark or some other area of law. There could be underlying copyright issues, but the predominant question might not be about copyright. Referral to the appropriate person on campus is the best way to respond or to recommend that the person seek outside private counsel. Referral to a local bar association is sometimes the best way to avoid any apparent conflict of interest or perceived bias toward a specific private attorney.
2. If it is a copyright question, then is it one of ownership or use? Sometimes it can be a combination of both, but it's best to first isolate them and address each one separately at least initially.
3. If it's an ownership question, then the status of ownership needs to be determined.
   a. Is it a work for hire or a jointly authored work? If so, does it meet all the requirements under the copyright law?
   b. Does ownership of the work have any preexisting conditions attached to it? One such example is a work that might have been created as part of a grant or contract where the work is required to be available in an open-access repository after a certain period of time.
   c. Did the author transfer the copyright to a third party? Authors tend to be unaware that many times they exchange their copyright in return for having their work published. If this is the situation, did they retain any rights? Did they negotiate changes to the contract with the publisher by attaching their own or a preexisting addenda such as the ones from CIC or SPARC?
4. If it is a use question, then the analysis becomes a two-pronged one. Is the work protected? How can the work be legally used?
5. The first prong of the analysis is to determine if the work is protected under the U.S. Copyright Act.
   a. Was the work published in the United States prior to 1923? If so, then it is in the public domain, since the copyright has expired and no further copyright analysis is needed.
   b. Is the work a U.S. federal government document? If it is, then unless there is some notice to the contrary, the work is in the public domain, since federal government works cannot be copyrighted under section 105 of the U.S. Copyright Act.

    c. Was the work published during 1923–1977? If so, did it have a copyright notice? The copyright notice is the word "copyright" or the copyright symbol, ©; the year of publication; and the copyright holder's name. If there is not a copyright notice attached to works published during those years, then the work is in the public domain for failure to comply with copyright requirements.

    d. Was the work published during 1923–1963? If so, was the copyright renewed? If the copyright was not renewed, which was a requirement in order to maintain copyright protection, then the copyright in the work has expired and the work is in the public domain. Stanford University has created a copyright renewal database[1] whereby a user can search to see if books published in the United States during those years had their copyright renewed.

    e. Does the work fall under one of the categories of protected works under section 102 of the U.S. Copyright Act? This includes literary works; musical works; dramatic works; pantomimes and choreographic works; pictorial, graphic, and sculptural works; motions pictures and other audiovisual works; sound recordings; and architectural works.

    f. Is the work creative and fixed in a tangible medium of expression?

6. If the work is protected, then the next step is to determine how the work will be used and what exceptions might apply. Is the work for teaching, libraries, or research, which results in a publication? Is it for a commercial venture?

7. If the work is for teaching, then is it for use in a face-to-face classroom, for a hybrid course, or for a distance education course? Sections 110(1) and 110(2) will dictate the terms of use for teaching. The fair-use exception might also apply.

8. Is this a question about using copyrighted works to create new works? This would be the time to apply the four-factor fair-use test to determine if such use would be permitted.

9. If it is a question on digitizing library materials, then section 108 specifies the conditions under which a work can be digitized if the libraries are doing the digitizing for works in their collection.

10. What types or formats of work will be used? Is it a video, an image, music, or text? There might be different restrictions or allowances based upon the format.

11. Is it a lawfully made work under the copyright law? If the work has not been lawfully made then none of the exceptions would apply.

The copyright officer needs to have the basic facts before making a determination as to whether or not the copyright law is even applicable and, if so, then what exceptions might lend themselves to the specific situation. It's always important to do a thorough analysis of the copyright issues and to remember that there will be times that the use is beyond the scope of the exceptions and permission must be obtained from the copyright holder.

## PROFESSIONAL BEST PRACTICES

There are many professional organizations that have developed best practices when using copyrighted works. This mostly revolves around the application of fair use in certain situations. The earliest one was developed in 2005 for documentary filmmakers. The most recent one under development is for the visual arts. The following is a list of best practices developed by practitioners for their discipline.

- *Code of Best Practices in Fair Use for Poetry*[2]—clarifies for poets how fair use can apply to quotes and excerpts as well as creating works in new media.
- *Code of Best Practices in Fair Use for OpenCouseWare*[3]—In 2002, the Massachusetts Institute of Technology developed open courses available to the world. Many other institutions jumped on board and began offering similar initiatives. This code helps guide those that want to provide free and open educational materials, which is part of the Open Educational Resource movement.
- *Code of Best Practices in Fair Use for Media Literacy Education*[4]— This assists educators in helping students access, analyze, and evaluate media messages. It is to encourage critical thinking by applying fair use to copyrighted works that can include images, audiovisual works, and digital works.
- *Best Practices in Fair Use of Dance-Related Materials*[5]—assists curators, librarians, and archivists in applying fair use to dance-related materials such as still and moving images, dance catalogs, and dance posters. This to help guide the preservation of materials documenting the legacy of dance.
- *Code of Best Practices in Fair Use for Academic and Research Libraries*[6]—This is one of the newest best practices codes and has the support of the Association of Research Libraries. Although aspects of it are controversial, it provides fair-use principles and limitations in areas commonly encountered by academic librarians.

This is not an exhaustive list of best practices promoted by professional organizations but an overview of ones that are referred to in academic circles.

A code that is currently in the beginning stages of development is by the College Art Association for the visual arts. A report on the process and issues was recently published and is receiving quite a bit of positive buzz.[7] It is important that the copyright officer is familiar with some of these codes since they are cropping up as defenses in litigation.

## TERMINATION RIGHTS

There are two sections of the U.S. Copyright Act that are causing many people to sit up and take notice. The reason being is that the sections did not really impact that many people until recent years. Sections 203 and 304 address the termination of rights that had been granted by authors to third parties.

The 1976 Copyright Act, which went into effect on January 1, 1978, included provisions that allowed copyright holders to regain their copyright after a certain period of time expires. Creators of copyrighted works will generally sign away their rights early in their careers in order to eke out a living without really knowing the true value of their work. This is considered an inequitable bargaining power. The idea behind sections 203 and 304 is to "give authors a second bite of the apple, a second chance to exploit the rights in and benefit from the works they created."[8] There are, of course, requirements that creators must follow, but in the end they can terminate the grant of rights to a third party and regain their copyright.

Section 203 is for transfers of copyright by the author made on or after January 1, 1978. They have thirty-five years from the date of publication or forty years from the date of the granting of copyright to notify the copyright holder that they will be terminating the transfer. Section 304 affects transfers made by the author before January 1, 1978. The termination can occur fifty-six years from the date the copyright is secured. Authors have a five-year period of termination. The termination notices must be served to the current copyright holder no later than two years before time expires and up to ten

**Table 10.1. §203 Termination Rights Timeline**

| If Published in | Termination Window | Must Submit No Later Than | Must Submit No Earlier Than |
|---|---|---|---|
| 1978 | 2013–2018 | 2016 | 2003 |
| 1979 | 2014–2019 | 2017 | 2004 |
| 1980 | 2015–2020 | 2018 | 2005 |
| 1981 | 2016–2021 | 2019 | 2006 |
| 1982 | 2017–2022 | 2020 | 2007 |
| 1983 | 2018–2023 | 2021 | 2008 |

years before the beginning of the five-year period. If authors do not exercise their termination rights within the allotted time periods, then they lose the rights to have the copyright revert back to them.

Authors cannot contract away their termination rights. A common scenario is for a publisher to include as one of their clauses in their contract with the author the agreement that the author will not terminate the grant of rights at a later date. This clause is invalid, since section 203 specifically states that the author retains the right to terminate "notwithstanding any agreement to the contrary." Again, this was added to protect an inexperienced author from signing away rights to a potentially valuable work.

If the original authors have died, then the heirs have the opportunity to stand in the deceased's stead and terminate the transfer. This is called the termination interest. However, this is limited to heirs, either individually or together, who own or are entitled to half the termination interest. The heirs would include the author's surviving spouse, children, and grandchildren. In the event that none of the heirs survive, then the termination interest would be given to the author's executor, administrator, personal representative, or trustee. The children of the legendary musician Ray Charles exercised their termination interest in their father's songs, which resulted in a lawsuit with their father's foundation. The foundation was to receive the income generated from the songs' copyright royalties.[9] The court sided with the children finding that the foundation had no standing under the U.S. Copyright Law termination clauses.

There are specific areas where termination rights are not applicable. One of the areas is work for hire agreements where the creator is not the owner of the copyrighted work but the employer or contractor is. Marvel recently won their case against Jack Kirby's heirs who had attempted to terminate Marvel's copyrights in major comic book heroes such as Spider-Man and the Incredible Hulk. The Second Circuit Court of Appeals ruled that the creations by Kirby were works for hire, thus negating any copyright ownership by Kirby and subsequent heirs.[10] Given the high monetary stakes involved with termination rights, work for hire situations are being carefully scrutinized to ensure that all criteria is met under the doctrine.

Termination rights do not extend to beneficiaries who receive the transfer in the author's will. The beneficiaries will retain the copyright for the length of the copyright and the author's heirs will not be able to assert control.

Derivative works that have already been created are not subject to termination rights. It is only the original work that the copyright owners or their heirs claim a reversion right to. However, no new derivative works can be created without a new agreement. There has been extensive litigation in this area involving the franchising of the cartoon characters Superman and Spider-Man. There have been questions and litigation surrounding the copyright ownership of Superman for decades. However, in a recent ruling DC Comics retained the copyright to Superman since the heirs could not meet the termination requirements.[11]

Foreign rights are not affected by the termination clauses. It impacts only the rights that arise under the U.S. Copyright Law. So, for example, if the author entered into an agreement with a non-U.S. publisher who is distributing the work outside the United States, then that agreement will not be subject to the termination clauses.

In order for a termination to be valid, in addition to the time constraints, the termination notice must be in writing and must be signed by the appropriate parties. There is no form offered by the U.S. Copyright Office that one can use, but the requirements for the termination notice can be found in the Code of Federal Regulations.[12] The terminations must be recorded with the U.S. Copyright Office for a small fee.

In 2013, the first terminations under section 203 became effective. Victor Willis, of the famous 1970s musical group The Village People, regained the copyright to the song "Y.M.C.A" as well as other songs he wrote when he was the lead singer for the group as a result of the termination clauses.[13] Willis has estimated that the annual revenue from the songs is in the millions.[14] It is estimated that nearly 10,000 authors, including Tom Petty, Kris Kristofferson, Billy Joel, and Bob Dylan have filed notices of termination for some of their most famous songs.[15] This is only one industry. Now imagine this playing out with movies, books, and so forth. The economic impact to such industries can be staggering. This does not only affect famous people but those in higher education as well. Faculty can terminate the grants they made early in their careers and regain their copyright. The termination clauses have the potential to shift the way early copyrights are handled and the copyright officer needs to be familiar with this hot topic.

## FUTURE OF COPYRIGHT

As discussed in earlier chapters, the register of the U.S. Copyright Office, Maria Pallante, has indicated a desire to have the current Copyright Act revised to more adequately reflect how copyright is used. To this end, Congress has begun hearings on the scope of fair use. The Library Copyright Alliance submitted a statement[16] supporting retaining fair use as is, since it provides flexibility to a wide group of consumers. Representative Bob Goodlatte, who is the House Judiciary chair, has called for comprehensive copyright reform and has held hearings on copyright policy during 2013 and more hearings are scheduled in 2014.[17] The overhaul of the Copyright Act is a momentous initiative and one that takes years to complete. However, the impetus is there with the backing of many different constituencies. Copyright officers need to make sure that their voices as representatives of their institutions are heard and to partner with like-minded professional organizations. The exceptions that have been carved out in the current law may not be perfect, but in many instances they do work because of their flexibility. As the wheels of Congress grind slowly toward a new copyright law, It will be a battle of the rights holders against the users of copyrighted works, and the stakes are very high for education.

Another area that has been repeatedly discussed in early chapters but bears mentioning once again is the open-access movement. This has great impact on how copyright is viewed and used. We are only at the beginning stages of requiring public access to federally funded research from all of the major federal agencies. Their policies will dictate and change how higher education responds to copyright challenges for obtaining federal funding for research projects and their output. The open sharing of data is also front and center in the debate. The Public Library of Science (PLOS) has released a revised data policy that went into effect on March 1, 2014. They are requiring authors to include a data availability statement for all research articles published by PLOS journals. "In line with Open Access to research articles themselves, PLOS strongly believes that to best foster scientific progress, the underlying data should be made freely available for researchers to use, wherever this is legal and ethical. . . . Our viewpoint is quite simple: ensuring access to the underlying data should be an intrinsic part of the scientific publishing process."[18] The copyrightability of data is confusing, contentious, and complex. Copyright officers will be navigating the open-access data landscape for years to come.

## CONCLUSION

Copyright impacts a broad array of areas in education, which have been highlighted in the previous chapters. "Indeed, working with copyright law in the context of applied situations is less of a quest for answers than it is a path that takes you toward a resolution, or at least a decision, about individual aspects of copyright."[19] Previous chapters have provided examples of typical questions received by a copyright office and some options for different approaches in analyzing them. This is not legal advice but legal information. As noted, each copyright situation is very fact specific and any legal advice on such situations should be provided from the institution's legal counsel.

There is increasingly a copyright tug of war going on between content owners and content users, which is shaping how the balance of rights is being viewed and legislated. "Managing copyright and the changing legal landscape for libraries is central to the library community's long-term survival."[20] In both the library environment and the university as a whole, managing copyrights to further the educational goals of teaching, learning, and research is critical to the success of faculty, students, administrators, and staff as well as their institutions. The copyright officer is a key player in facilitating such successes.

## NOTES

1. Stanford University, "Copyright Renewal Database," *Libraries & Academic Information Resources*, accessed April 10, 2014, http://collections.stanford.edu/copy rightrenewals/bin/page?forward=home.

2. Center for Social Media, *Code of Best Practices in Fair Use for Poetry* (Washington, DC: Center for Social Media, 2011), accessed April 10, 2014, http://www .cmsimpact.org/sites/default/files/documents/pages/fairusepoetrybooklet_single pg_3.pdf.

3. Center for Social Media, *Code of Best Practices in Fair Use for OpenCourse-Ware* (Washington, DC: Center for Social Media, 2009), accessed April 10, 2014, http://www.cmsimpact.org/sites/default/files/10-305-OCW-Oct29.pdf.

4. Center for Social Media, *Code of Best Practices in Fair Use for Media Literacy Education* (Washington, DC: Center for Social Media, 2008), accessed April 10, 2014, http://mediaeducationlab.com/sites/mediaeducationlab.com/files/CodeofBest PracticesinFairUse_0.pdf.

5. Dance Heritage Coalition, *Best Practices in Fair Use of Dance-Related Materials* (Washington, DC: Dance Heritage Coalition, 2010), accessed April 10, 2014, http://www.cmsimpact.org/sites/default/files/documents/pages/DHC_fair_use_state ment.pdf.

6. Association of Research Libraries, "Code of Best Practices in Fair Use for Academic and Research Libraries," *Association of Research Libraries*, January 2012, accessed April 10, 2014, http://www.arl.org/storage/documents/publications/code-of -best-practices-fair-use.pdf.

7. Patricia Aufderheide, Peter Jaszi, Bryan Bello, and Tijana Milosevic, "Copyright, Permissions, and Fair Use among Visual Artists and the Academic and Museum Visual Arts Communities: An Issues Report," *College Art Association*, February 2014, accessed April 10, 2014, http://www.collegeart.org/pdf/FairUseIssuesReport .pdf.

8. Margo E. Crespin, *A Second Bite of the Apple: A Guide to Terminating Transfers under Section 203 of the Copyright Act* (New York: The Authors Guild, 2005), accessed April 10, 2014, http://www.authorsguild.org/services/legal-services/ terminating-transfers/.

9. Kevin Park, "From Ray Charles to 'Y.M.C.A.'—Section 203 Copyright Terminations in 2013 and Beyond," *The IP Litigator: Devoted to Intellectual Property Litigation and Enforcement* 19 no. 2 (Mar/Apr 2013): 7–12.

10. "Marvel to Keep Spider-Man, X-Men Rights after Family of Original Artist Sues to Terminate Comic Giant's Copyrights—Agree Work Was 'For Hire,'" *New York Post*, August 8, 2013, accessed April 10, 2014, http://nypost.com/2013/08/08/marvel-to-keep-spider-man-x-men-rights-after-family-of-original-artist-sues-to-terminate-comic-giants-copyrights-agree-work-was-for-hire/.

11. Joe Mullin, "Heirs of Superman Artist Can't Reclaim Their Copyright, Judge Rules," *Arts Technica*, October 18, 2012, accessed April 10, 2014, http://arstechnica.com/tech-policy/2012/10/heirs-of-superman-artist-cant-reclaim-their-copyright-judge-rules/.

12. Notices of Termination of Transfer and Licenses, 37 C.F.R. section 201.10.

13. Larry Rohter, "A Copyright Victory 35 Years Later," *New York Times*, September 10, 2013, accessed April 10, 2014, http://www.nytimes.com/2013/09/11/arts/music/a-copyright-victory-35-years-later.html?_r=0.

14. Park, "From Ray Charles to 'Y.M.C.A.,'" 9.

15. Park, "From Ray Charles to 'Y.M.C.A.,'" 10.

16. Library Copyright Alliance, "Before the House Committee on the Judiciary Subcommittee on Courts, Intellectual Property and the Internet; Hearing on the Scope of Fair Use: Statement of the Library Copyright Alliance," January 28, 2014, accessed April 10, 2014, http://www.librarycopyrightalliance.org/bm~doc/stfairusepsarev.pdf.

17. Leigh Beadon, "Bob Goodlatte Calls for Copyright Reform, Leaves Specifics to the Imagination," *Techdirt*, April 24, 2013, accessed April 10, 2014, http://www.techdirt.com/articles/20130424/13183222824/bob-goodlatte-calls-copyright-reform-leaves-specifics-to-imagination.shtml.

18. Theo Bloom, "Data Access for the Open Access Literature: PLOS's Data Policy," *PLOS*, December 12, 2013, accessed April 10, 2014, http://www.plos.org/data-access-for-the-open-access-literature-ploss-data-policy/.

19. Kenneth D. Crews, *Copyright Law for Librarians and Educators: Creative Strategies and Practical Solutions* (Chicago: American Library Association, 2012).

20. Dwayne K. Buttler, "Intimacy Gone Awry: Copyright and Special Collections," *Journal of Library Administration* 52 (2012): 279–93.

# Appendix A

## U.S. Copyright Law, Sections 106–110

### § 106. EXCLUSIVE RIGHTS IN COPYRIGHTED WORKS

Subject to sections 107 through 122, the owner of copyright under this title has the exclusive rights to do and to authorize any of the following:

(1) to reproduce the copyrighted work in copies or phonorecords;
(2) to prepare derivative works based upon the copyrighted work;
(3) to distribute copies or phonorecords of the copyrighted work to the public by sale or other transfer of ownership, or by rental, lease, or lending;
(4) in the case of literary, musical, dramatic, and choreographic works, pantomimes, and motion pictures and other audiovisual works, to perform the copyrighted work publicly;
(5) in the case of literary, musical, dramatic, and choreographic works, pantomimes, and pictorial, graphic, or sculptural works, including the individual images of a motion picture or other audiovisual work, to display the copyrighted work publicly; and
(6) in the case of sound recordings, to perform the copyrighted work publicly by means of a digital audio transmission.

### § 107. LIMITATIONS ON EXCLUSIVE RIGHTS: FAIR USE

Notwithstanding the provisions of sections 106 and 106A, the fair use of a copyrighted work, including such use by reproduction in copies or phonorecords or by any other means specified by that section, for purposes such as criticism, comment, news reporting, teaching (including multiple copies for classroom use), scholarship, or research, is not an infringement of copyright. In determining whether the use made of a work in any particular case is a fair use the factors to be considered shall include—

(1) the purpose and character of the use, including whether such use is of a commercial nature or is for nonprofit educational purposes;
(2) the nature of the copyrighted work;
(3) the amount and substantiality of the portion used in relation to the copyrighted work as a whole; and
(4) the effect of the use upon the potential market for or value of the copyrighted work.

The fact that a work is unpublished shall not itself bar a finding of fair use if such finding is made upon consideration of all the above factors.

## § 108. LIMITATIONS ON EXCLUSIVE RIGHTS: REPRODUCTION BY LIBRARIES AND ARCHIVES

(a) Except as otherwise provided in this title and notwithstanding the provisions of section 106, it is not an infringement of copyright for a library or archives, or any of its employees acting within the scope of their employment, to reproduce no more than one copy or phonorecord of a work, except as provided in subsections (b) and (c), or to distribute such copy or phonorecord, under the conditions specified by this section, if—

(1) the reproduction or distribution is made without any purpose of direct or indirect commercial advantage;
(2) the collections of the library or archives are (i) open to the public, or (ii) available not only to researchers affiliated with the library or archives or with the institution of which it is a part, but also to other persons doing research in a specialized field; and
(3) the reproduction or distribution of the work includes a notice of copyright that appears on the copy or phonorecord that is reproduced under the provisions of this section, or includes a legend stating that the work may be protected by copyright if no such notice can be found on the copy or phonorecord that is reproduced under the provisions of this section.

(b) The rights of reproduction and distribution under this section apply to three copies or phonorecords of an unpublished work duplicated solely for purposes of preservation and security or for deposit for research use in another library or archives of the type described by clause (2) of subsection (a), if—

    (1) the copy or phonorecord reproduced is currently in the collections of the library or archives; and

    (2) any such copy or phonorecord that is reproduced in digital format is not otherwise distributed in that format and is not made available to the public in that format outside the premises of the library or archives.

(c) The right of reproduction under this section applies to three copies or phonorecords of a published work duplicated solely for the purpose of replacement of a copy or phonorecord that is damaged, deteriorating, lost, or stolen, or if the existing format in which the work is stored has become obsolete, if—

    (1) the library or archives has, after a reasonable effort, determined that an unused replacement cannot be obtained at a fair price; and

    (2) any such copy or phonorecord that is reproduced in digital format is not made available to the public in that format outside the premises of the library or archives in lawful possession of such copy.

    For purposes of this subsection, a format shall be considered obsolete if the machine or device necessary to render perceptible a work stored in that format is no longer manufactured or is no longer reasonably available in the commercial marketplace.

(d) The rights of reproduction and distribution under this section apply to a copy, made from the collection of a library or archives where the user makes his or her request or from that of another library or archives, of no more than one article or other contribution to a copyrighted collection or periodical issue, or to a copy or phonorecord of a small part of any other copyrighted work, if—

    (1) the copy or phonorecord becomes the property of the user, and the library or archives has had no notice that the copy or phonorecord would be used for any purpose other than private study, scholarship, or research; and

    (2) the library or archives displays prominently, at the place where orders are accepted, and includes on its order form, a warning of copyright in accordance with requirements that the Register of Copyrights shall prescribe by regulation.

(e) The rights of reproduction and distribution under this section apply to the entire work, or to a substantial part of it, made from the collection of a library or archives where the user makes his or her request or from that of another library or archives, if the library or archives has first determined, on the basis of a reasonable investigation, that a copy or phonorecord of the copyrighted work cannot be obtained at a fair price, if—

(1) the copy or phonorecord becomes the property of the user, and the library or archives has had no notice that the copy or phonorecord would be used for any purpose other than private study, scholarship, or research; and

(2) the library or archives displays prominently, at the place where orders are accepted, and includes on its order form, a warning of copyright in accordance with requirements that the Register of Copyrights shall prescribe by regulation.

(f) Nothing in this section—

(1) shall be construed to impose liability for copyright infringement upon a library or archives or its employees for the unsupervised use of reproducing equipment located on its premises: Provided, That such equipment displays a notice that the making of a copy may be subject to the copyright law;

(2) excuses a person who uses such reproducing equipment or who requests a copy or phonorecord under subsection (d) from liability for copyright infringement for any such act, or for any later use of such copy or phonorecord, if it exceeds fair use as provided by section 107;

(3) shall be construed to limit the reproduction and distribution by lending of a limited number of copies and excerpts by a library or archives of an audiovisual news program, subject to clauses (1), (2), and (3) of subsection (a); or

(4) in any way affects the right of fair use as provided by section 107, or any contractual obligations assumed at any time by the library or archives when it obtained a copy or phonorecord of a work in its collections.

(g) The rights of reproduction and distribution under this section extend to the isolated and unrelated reproduction or distribution of a single copy or phonorecord of the same material on separate occasions, but do not extend to cases where the library or archives, or its employee—

(1) is aware or has substantial reason to believe that it is engaging in the related or concerted reproduction or distribution of multiple copies or phonorecords of the same material, whether made on one occasion or over a period of time, and whether intended for aggregate use by one or more individuals or for separate use by the individual members of a group; or

(2) engages in the systematic reproduction or distribution of single or multiple copies or phonorecords of material described in subsection (d): Provided, That nothing in this clause prevents a library or archives from participating in interlibrary arrangements that do not have, as their purpose or effect, that the library or archives receiving such cop-

ies or phonorecords for distribution does so in such aggregate quantities as to substitute for a subscription to or purchase of such work.

(h)
(1) For purposes of this section, during the last 20 years of any term of copyright of a published work, a library or archives, including a non-profit educational institution that functions as such, may reproduce, distribute, display, or perform in facsimile or digital form a copy or phonorecord of such work, or portions thereof, for purposes of preservation, scholarship, or research, if such library or archives has first determined, on the basis of a reasonable investigation, that none of the conditions set forth in subparagraphs (A), (B), and (C) of paragraph (2) apply.

(2) No reproduction, distribution, display, or performance is authorized under this subsection if—

(A) the work is subject to normal commercial exploitation;

(B) a copy or phonorecord of the work can be obtained at a reasonable price; or

(C) the copyright owner or its agent provides notice pursuant to regulations promulgated by the Register of Copyrights that either of the conditions set forth in subparagraphs (A) and (B) applies.

(3) The exemption provided in this subsection does not apply to any subsequent uses by users other than such library or archives.

(i) The rights of reproduction and distribution under this section do not apply to a musical work, a pictorial, graphic or sculptural work, or a motion picture or other audiovisual work other than an audiovisual work dealing with news, except that no such limitation shall apply with respect to rights granted by subsections (b), (c), and (h), or with respect to pictorial or graphic works published as illustrations, diagrams, or similar adjuncts to works of which copies are reproduced or distributed in accordance with subsections (d) and (e).

## § 109. LIMITATIONS ON EXCLUSIVE RIGHTS: EFFECT OF TRANSFER OF PARTICULAR COPY OR PHONORECORD

(a) Notwithstanding the provisions of section 106(3), the owner of a particular copy or phonorecord lawfully made under this title, or any person authorized by such owner, is entitled, without the authority of the copyright owner, to sell or otherwise dispose of the possession of that copy or phonorecord. Notwithstanding the preceding sentence, copies or phonorecords of works subject to restored copyright under section 104A that are manufactured before the date of restoration of copyright or, with respect to reliance parties, before publication or service of notice under section 104A(e), may be sold or otherwise disposed of without the authorization of the owner of the restored copyright for purposes of direct or indirect commercial advantage only during the 12-month period beginning on—

    (1) the date of the publication in the Federal Register of the notice of intent filed with the Copyright Office under section 104A(d)(2)(A), or

    (2) the date of the receipt of actual notice served under section 104A(d)(2)(B), whichever occurs first.

(b)

  (1)

    (A) Notwithstanding the provisions of subsection (a), unless authorized by the owners of copyright in the sound recording or the owner of copyright in a computer program (including any tape, disk, or other medium embodying such program), and in the case of a sound recording in the musical works embodied therein, neither the owner of a particular phonorecord nor any person in possession of a particular copy of a computer program (including any tape, disk, or other medium embodying such program), may, for the purposes of direct or indirect commercial advantage, dispose of, or authorize the disposal of, the possession of that phonorecord or computer program (including any tape, disk, or other medium embodying such program) by rental, lease, or lending, or by any other act or practice in the nature of rental, lease, or lending. Nothing in the preceding sentence shall apply to the rental, lease, or lending of a phonorecord for nonprofit purposes by a nonprofit library or nonprofit educational institution. The transfer of possession of a lawfully made copy of a computer program by a nonprofit educational institution to another nonprofit educational institution or to faculty, staff, and students does not constitute rental, lease, or lending for direct or indirect commercial purposes under this subsection.

    (B) This subsection does not apply to—

      (i) a computer program which is embodied in a machine or product and which cannot be copied during the ordinary operation or use of the machine or product; or

     (ii) a computer program embodied in or used in conjunction with a limited purpose computer that is designed for playing video games and may be designed for other purposes.

    (C) Nothing in this subsection affects any provision of chapter 9 of this title.

(2)

(A) Nothing in this subsection shall apply to the lending of a computer program for nonprofit purposes by a nonprofit library, if each copy of a computer program which is lent by such library has affixed to the packaging containing the program a warning of copyright in accordance with requirements that the Register of Copyrights shall prescribe by regulation.

(B) Not later than three years after the date of the enactment of the Computer Software Rental Amendments Act of 1990, and at such times thereafter as the Register of Copyrights considers appropriate, the Register of Copyrights, after consultation with representatives of copyright owners and librarians, shall submit to the Congress a report stating whether this paragraph has achieved its intended purpose of maintaining the integrity of the copyright system while providing nonprofit libraries the capability to fulfill their function. Such report shall advise the Congress as to any information or recommendations that the Register of Copyrights considers necessary to carry out the purposes of this subsection.

(3) Nothing in this subsection shall affect any provision of the antitrust laws. For purposes of the preceding sentence, "antitrust laws" has the meaning given that term in the first section of the Clayton Act and includes section 5 of the Federal Trade Commission Act to the extent that section relates to unfair methods of competition.

(4) Any person who distributes a phonorecord or a copy of a computer program (including any tape, disk, or other medium embodying such program) in violation of paragraph (1) is an infringer of copyright under section 501 of this title and is subject to the remedies set forth in sections 502, 503, 504, and 505. Such violation shall not be a criminal offense under section 506 or cause such person to be subject to the criminal penalties set forth in section 2319 of title 18.

(c) Notwithstanding the provisions of section 106(5), the owner of a particular copy lawfully made under this title, or any person authorized by such owner, is entitled, without the authority of the copyright owner, to display that copy publicly, either directly or by the projection of no more than one image at a time, to viewers present at the place where the copy is located.

(d) The privileges prescribed by subsections (a) and (c) do not, unless authorized by the copyright owner, extend to any person who has acquired possession of the copy or phonorecord from the copyright owner, by rental, lease, loan, or otherwise, without acquiring ownership of it.

(e) Notwithstanding the provisions of sections 106(4) and 106(5), in the case of an electronic audiovisual game intended for use in coin-operated equipment, the owner of a particular copy of such a game lawfully made under this title, is entitled, without the authority of the copyright owner of the game, to publicly perform or display that game in coin-operated equipment, except that this subsection shall not apply to any work of authorship embodied in the audiovisual game if the copyright owner of the electronic audiovisual game is not also the copyright owner of the work of authorship.

## § 110. LIMITATIONS ON EXCLUSIVE RIGHTS: EXEMPTION OF CERTAIN PERFORMANCES AND DISPLAYS

Notwithstanding the provisions of section 106, the following are not infringements of copyright:

(1) performance or display of a work by instructors or pupils in the course of face-to-face teaching activities of a nonprofit educational institution, in a classroom or similar place devoted to instruction, unless, in the case of a motion picture or other audiovisual work, the performance, or the display of individual images, is given by means of a copy that was not lawfully made under this title, and that the person responsible for the performance knew or had reason to believe was not lawfully made;

(2) except with respect to a work produced or marketed primarily for performance or display as part of mediated instructional activities transmitted via digital networks, or a performance or display that is given by means of a copy or phonorecord that is not lawfully made and acquired under this title, and the transmitting government body or accredited nonprofit educational institution knew or had reason to believe was not lawfully made and acquired, the performance of a nondramatic literary or musical work or reasonable and limited portions of any other work, or display of a work in an amount comparable to that which is typically displayed in the course of a live classroom session, by or in the course of a transmission, if—

   (A) the performance or display is made by, at the direction of, or under the actual supervision of an instructor as an integral part of a class session offered as a regular part of the systematic mediated instructional activities of a governmental body or an accredited nonprofit educational institution;

   (B) the performance or display is directly related and of material assistance to the teaching content of the transmission;

   (C) the transmission is made solely for, and, to the extent technologically feasible, the reception of such transmission is limited to—

(i) students officially enrolled in the course for which the transmission is made; or

(ii) officers or employees of governmental bodies as a part of their official duties or employment; and

(D) the transmitting body or institution—

(i) institutes policies regarding copyright, provides informational materials to faculty, students, and relevant staff members that accurately describe, and promote compliance with, the laws of the United States relating to copyright, and provides notice to students that materials used in connection with the course may be subject to copyright protection; and

(ii) in the case of digital transmissions—

(I) applies technological measures that reasonably prevent—

(aa) retention of the work in accessible form by recipients of the transmission from the transmitting body or institution for longer than the class session; and

(bb) unauthorized further dissemination of the work in accessible form by such recipients to others; and

(II) does not engage in conduct that could reasonably be expected to interfere with technological measures used by copyright owners to prevent such retention or unauthorized further dissemination;

(3) performance of a nondramatic literary or musical work or of a dramatico-musical work of a religious nature, or display of a work, in the course of services at a place of worship or other religious assembly;

(4) performance of a nondramatic literary or musical work otherwise than in a transmission to the public, without any purpose of direct or indirect commercial advantage and without payment of any fee or other compensation for the performance to any of its performers, promoters, or organizers, if—

(A) there is no direct or indirect admission charge; or

(B) the proceeds, after deducting the reasonable costs of producing the performance, are used exclusively for educational, religious, or charitable purposes and not for private financial gain, except where the copyright owner has served notice of objection to the performance under the following conditions:

(i) the notice shall be in writing and signed by the copyright owner or such owner's duly authorized agent; and

(ii) the notice shall be served on the person responsible for the performance at least seven days before the date of the performance, and shall state the reasons for the objection; and

    (iii) the notice shall comply, in form, content, and manner of service, with requirements that the Register of Copyrights shall prescribe by regulation;

(5)

  (A) except as provided in subparagraph (B), communication of a transmission embodying a performance or display of a work by the public reception of the transmission on a single receiving apparatus of a kind commonly used in private homes, unless—

    (i) a direct charge is made to see or hear the transmission; or

    (ii) the transmission thus received is further transmitted to the public;

  (B) communication by an establishment of a transmission or retransmission embodying a performance or display of a nondramatic musical work intended to be received by the general public, originated by a radio or television broadcast station licensed as such by the Federal Communications Commission, or, if an audiovisual transmission, by a cable system or satellite carrier, if—

    (i) in the case of an establishment other than a food service or drinking establishment, either the establishment in which the communication occurs has less than 2,000 gross square feet of space (excluding space used for customer parking and for no other purpose), or the establishment in which the communication occurs has 2,000 or more gross square feet of space (excluding space used for customer parking and for no other purpose) and—

      (I) if the performance is by audio means only, the performance is communicated by means of a total of not more than 6 loudspeakers, of which not more than 4 loudspeakers are located in any 1 room or adjoining outdoor space; or

      (II) if the performance or display is by audiovisual means, any visual portion of the performance or display is communicated by means of a total of not more than 4 audiovisual devices, of which not more than 1 audiovisual device is located in any 1 room, and no such audiovisual device has a diagonal screen size greater than 55 inches, and any audio portion of the performance or display is communicated by means of a total of not more than 6 loudspeakers, of which not more than 4 loudspeakers are located in any 1 room or adjoining outdoor space;

    (ii) in the case of a food service or drinking establishment, either the establishment in which the communication occurs has less than 3,750 gross square feet of space (excluding space used for customer parking and for no other purpose), or the establishment in which the communication occurs has 3,750 gross square feet of space or more (excluding space used for customer parking and for no other purpose) and—

(I) if the performance is by audio means only, the performance is communicated by means of a total of not more than 6 loudspeakers, of which not more than 4 loudspeakers are located in any 1 room or adjoining outdoor space; or

(II) if the performance or display is by audiovisual means, any visual portion of the performance or display is communicated by means of a total of not more than 4 audiovisual devices, of which not more than 1 audiovisual device is located in any 1 room, and no such audiovisual device has a diagonal screen size greater than 55 inches, and any audio portion of the performance or display is communicated by means of a total of not more than 6 loudspeakers, of which not more than 4 loudspeakers are located in any 1 room or adjoining outdoor space;

(iii) no direct charge is made to see or hear the transmission or retransmission;

(iv) the transmission or retransmission is not further transmitted beyond the establishment where it is received; and

(v) the transmission or retransmission is licensed by the copyright owner of the work so publicly performed or displayed;

(6) performance of a nondramatic musical work by a governmental body or a nonprofit agricultural or horticultural organization, in the course of an annual agricultural or horticultural fair or exhibition conducted by such body or organization; the exemption provided by this clause shall extend to any liability for copyright infringement that would otherwise be imposed on such body or organization, under doctrines of vicarious liability or related infringement, for a performance by a concessionaire, business establishment, or other person at such fair or exhibition, but shall not excuse any such person from liability for the performance;

(7) performance of a nondramatic musical work by a vending establishment open to the public at large without any direct or indirect admission charge, where the sole purpose of the performance is to promote the retail sale of copies or phonorecords of the work, or of the audiovisual or other devices utilized in such performance, and the performance is not transmitted beyond the place where the establishment is located and is within the immediate area where the sale is occurring;

(8) performance of a nondramatic literary work, by or in the course of a transmission specifically designed for and primarily directed to blind or other handicapped persons who are unable to read normal printed material as a result of their handicap, or deaf or other handicapped persons who are unable to hear the aural signals accompanying a transmission of visual signals, if the performance is made without any purpose of direct or indirect commercial advantage and its transmission is made through the facilities of: (i) a governmental body; or (ii) a noncommercial educational broadcast station (as defined in section 397 of title 47); or (iii) a radio subcarrier authorization (as defined in 47 CFR 73.293–73.295 and 73.593–73.595); or (iv) a cable system (as defined in section 111 (f));

(9) performance on a single occasion of a dramatic literary work published at least ten years before the date of the performance, by or in the course of a transmission specifically designed for and primarily directed to blind or other handicapped persons who are unable to read normal printed material as a result of their handicap, if the performance is made without any purpose of direct or indirect commercial advantage and its transmission is made through the facilities of a radio subcarrier authorization referred to in clause (8) (iii), Provided, That the provisions of this clause shall not be applicable to more than one performance of the same work by the same performers or under the auspices of the same organization;

(10) notwithstanding paragraph (4), the following is not an infringement of copyright: performance of a nondramatic literary or musical work in the course of a social function which is organized and promoted by a nonprofit veterans' organization or a nonprofit fraternal organization to which the general public is not invited, but not including the invitees of the organizations, if the proceeds from the performance, after deducting the reasonable costs of producing the performance, are used exclusively for charitable purposes and not for financial gain. For purposes of this section the social functions of any college or university fraternity or sorority shall not be included unless the social function is held solely to raise funds for a specific charitable purpose; and

(11) the making imperceptible, by or at the direction of a member of a private household, of limited portions of audio or video content of a motion picture, during a performance in or transmitted to that household for private home viewing, from an authorized copy of the motion picture, or the creation or provision of a computer program or other technology that enables such making imperceptible and that is

designed and marketed to be used, at the direction of a member of a private household, for such making imperceptible, if no fixed copy of the altered version of the motion picture is created by such computer program or other technology.

The exemptions provided under paragraph (5) shall not be taken into account in any administrative, judicial, or other governmental proceeding to set or adjust the royalties payable to copyright owners for the public performance or display of their works. Royalties payable to copyright owners for any public performance or display of their works other than such performances or displays as are exempted under paragraph (5) shall not be diminished in any respect as a result of such exemption.

In paragraph (2), the term "mediated instructional activities" with respect to the performance or display of a work by digital transmission under this section refers to activities that use such work as an integral part of the class experience, controlled by or under the actual supervision of the instructor and analogous to the type of performance or display that would take place in a live classroom setting. The term does not refer to activities that use, in 1 or more class sessions of a single course, such works as textbooks, course packs, or other material in any media, copies or phonorecords of which are typically purchased or acquired by the students in higher education for their independent use and retention or are typically purchased or acquired for elementary and secondary students for their possession and independent use.

For purposes of paragraph (2), accreditation—

(A) with respect to an institution providing post-secondary education, shall be as determined by a regional or national accrediting agency recognized by the Council on Higher Education Accreditation or the United States Department of Education; and

(B) with respect to an institution providing elementary or secondary education, shall be as recognized by the applicable state certification or licensing procedures.

For purposes of paragraph (2), no governmental body or accredited nonprofit educational institution shall be liable for infringement by reason of the transient or temporary storage of material carried out through the automatic technical process of a digital transmission of the performance or display of that material as authorized under paragraph (2). No such material stored on the system or network controlled or operated by the transmitting body or institution under this paragraph shall be maintained on such system or network in a manner ordinarily accessible to anyone other than anticipated recipients. No such copy shall be maintained on the system or network in a manner ordinarily accessible to such anticipated recipients for a longer period than is reasonably necessary to facilitate the transmissions for which it was made.

For purposes of paragraph (11), the term "making imperceptible" does not include the addition of audio or video content that is performed or displayed over or in place of existing content in a motion picture.

Nothing in paragraph (11) shall be construed to imply further rights under section 106 of this title, or to have any effect on defenses or limitations on rights granted under any other section of this title or under any other paragraph of this section.

# Appendix B

## Fair-Use Checklist

### FAIR-USE CHECKLIST INTRODUCTION
### BY: KENNETH D. CREWS

The Fair-Use Checklist and variations on it have been widely used for many years to help educators, librarians, lawyers, and many other users of copyrighted works determine whether their activities are within the limits of fair use under U.S. copyright law (Section 107 of the U.S. Copyright Act). Fair use is determined by a balanced application of four factors set forth in the statute: (1) the purpose of the use; (2) the nature of the work used; (3) the amount and substantiality of the work used; and (4) the effect of the use upon the potential market for or value of the work used. Those factors form the structure of this checklist. Congress and courts have offered some insights into the specific meaning of the factors, and those interpretations are reflected in the details of this form.

### Benefits of the Checklist

A proper use of this checklist should serve two purposes. First, it should help you to focus on factual circumstances that are important in your evaluation of fair use. The meaning and scope of fair use depends on the particular facts of a given situation, and changing one or more facts may alter the analysis. Second, the checklist can provide an important mechanism to document your decision-making process. Maintaining a record of your fair-use analysis can be critical for establishing good faith; consider adding to the checklist the current date and notes about your project. Keep completed checklists on file for future reference.

**The Checklist as Roadmap**

As you use the checklist and apply it to your situations, you are likely to check more than one box in each column and even check boxes across columns. Some checked boxes will favor fair use and others may oppose fair use. A key issue is whether you are acting reasonably in checking any given box, with the ultimate question being whether the cumulative weight of the factors favors or turns you away from fair use. This is not an exercise in simply checking and counting boxes. Instead, you need to consider the relative persuasive strength of the circumstances and if the overall conditions lean most convincingly for or against fair use. Because you are most familiar with your project, you are probably best positioned to evaluate the facts and make the decision.

**Fair Use Checklist**
Copyright Advisory Office
Columbia University Libraries
Kenneth D. Crews, Director
http://copyright.columbia.edu

| | |
|---|---|
| Name: | |
| Institution: | |
| Project: | |
| Date: | |
| Prepared by: | |

## Purpose

**Favoring Fair Use**

- ☐ Teaching (including multiple copies for classroom use)
- ☐ Research
- ☐ Scholarship
- ☐ Nonprofit educational institution
- ☐ Criticism
- ☐ Comment
- ☐ News reporting
- ☐ Transformative or productive use (changes the work for new utility)
- ☐ Restricted access (to students or other appropriate group)
- ☐ Parody

**Opposing Fair Use**

- ☐ Commercial activity
- ☐ Profiting from the use
- ☐ Entertainment
- ☐ Bad-faith behavior
- ☐ Denying credit to original author

## Nature

**Favoring Fair Use**

☐ Published work

☐ Factual or nonfiction based

☐ Important to favored educational objectives

**Opposing Fair Use**

☐ Unpublished work

☐ Highly creative work (art, music, novels, films, plays)

☐ Fiction

## Amount

**Favoring Fair Use**

☐ Small quantity

☐ Portion used is not central or significant to entire work

☐ Amount is appropriate for favored educational purpose

**Opposing Fair Use**

☐ Large portion or whole work used

☐ Portion used is central to or "heart of the work"

## Effect

**Favoring Fair Use**

☐ User owns lawfully purchased or acquired copy of original work

☐ One or few copies made

☐ No significant effect on the market or potential market for copyrighted work

☐ No similar product marketed by the copyright holder

☐ Lack of licensing mechanism

**Opposing Fair Use**

☐ Could replace sale of copyrighted work

☐ Significantly impairs market or potential market for copyrighted work or derivative

☐ Reasonably available licensing mechanism for use of the copyrighted work

☐ Affordable permission available for using work

☐ Numerous copies made

☐ You made it accessible on the Web or in other public forum

☐ Repeated or long-term use

# Appendix C

CIC Statement on Publishing Agreements

C·I·C

### The Committee on Institutional Cooperation (CIC)
### STATEMENT ON PUBLISHING AGREEMENTS

*The Committee on Institutional Cooperation (CIC)[1] is a consortium of 15 world-class American research universities, advancing their missions by sharing expertise, leveraging campus resources and collaborating on innovative programs. For 50 years, the CIC has created new opportunities for member universities to work together toward greater efficiency, effectiveness and impact. In 2006, the Provosts of the CIC member universities unanimously endorsed this statement and addendum to publication agreements. Since that time, faculty governance of 12 CIC campuses[2] have also endorsed the statement and addendum.*

Publication is the lifeblood of a research university. It is incumbent upon faculty, campus administrators and librarians to ensure the free flow of scholarly information in fulfillment of our campus missions to advance the public good through research and education. Toward this end, our campuses are committed to supporting a sustainable publication process and a healthy publishing industry. The "information revolution" has greatly expanded the means for disseminating and utilizing scholarly discourse, but this opportunity for extending the reach and impact of our campuses is countered by social and economic conventions of some sectors of the publishing industry. Suitable publishing partners for academic enterprises should be encouraging the widest possible dissemination of the academy's work, and the management of copyright should be directed to encouraging scholarly output rather than unnecessarily fettering its access and use. Without some important changes in publishing practices, authors and readers will continue to be frustrated by barriers to the free flow of information that is an essential characteristic of great research universities.

Faculty authors should consider a number of factors when choosing and interacting with publishers for their works. The goal of publication should be to encourage widespread dissemination and impact; the means for accomplishing this will necessarily depend on the nature of the work in question, the author's circumstances, available suitable outlets, and expectations in the author's field of inquiry. In general, authors are encouraged to consider publishing strategies that will optimize short- and long-term access to their work, taking into account such factors as affordability, efficient means for distribution, a secure third-party archiving strategy, and flexible management of rights.

Protecting intellectual property rights is a particularly important consideration, as many authors unwittingly sign away all control over their creative output. Toward this end, the CIC encourages contract language that ensures that academic authors retain certain rights that facilitate archiving, instructional use, and sharing with colleagues to advance discourse and discovery. Accompanying this document is a model CIC publishing addendum that affirms the rights of authors to share their work in a variety of circumstances, including posting versions of the work in institutional or disciplinary repositories. While the particular circumstances and terms governing publication will vary on a case-by-case basis, the underlying principle of encouraging access to the creative output of our campuses should inhere in all of our efforts.

[1] The 15 CIC member universities are: University of Chicago; University of Illinois; Indiana University; University of Iowa; University of Maryland; University of Michigan; Michigan State University; University of Minnesota; University of Nebraska-Lincoln; Northwestern University; The Ohio State University; The Pennsylvania State University; Purdue University; Rutgers University; University of Wisconsin-Madison

[2] As of June 5, 2008, faculty governance from the following CIC universities have endorsed the statement and addendum: University of Illinois (both the Chicago and the Urbana-Champaign campuses), Indiana University; University of Iowa, University of Michigan; Michigan State University; University of Minnesota; Northwestern University; The Pennsylvania State University, The Ohio State University; Purdue University; and the University of Wisconsin-Madison

### Courtesy of the Committee on Institutional Cooperation

## ADDENDUM TO PUBLICATION AGREEMENTS FOR CIC[3] AUTHORS

This ADDENDUM hereby modifies and supplements the attached Publication Agreement between:

Corresponding Author _____

Additional Authors (if any) _____

_____

AND

Publisher _____

Related to Manuscript titled _____

_____

To appear in Journal, Anthology, or Collection titled _____

_____

PUBLISHER AND AUTHOR AGREE THAT WHERE THERE ARE CONFLICTING TERMS BETWEEN THE PUBLICATION AGREEMENT AND THIS ADDENDUM, THE PROVISIONS OF THIS ADDENDUM WILL BE PARAMOUNT. IN ADDITION TO THE RIGHTS GRANTED THE AUTHOR IN THE PUBLICATION AGREEMENT AND BY LAW, THE PARTIES AGREE THAT THE AUTHOR SHALL ALSO RETAIN THE FOLLOWING SPECIFIED RIGHTS:

1. The Author shall, without limitation, have the non-exclusive right to use, reproduce, distribute, and create derivative works including update, perform, and display publicly, the Article in electronic, digital or print form in connection with the Author's teaching, conference presentations, lectures, other scholarly works, and for all of Author's academic and professional activities.

2. After a period of six(6) months from the date of publication of the article, the Author shall also have all the non-exclusive rights necessary to make, or to authorize others to make, the final published version of the Article available in digital form over the Internet, including but not limited to a website under the control of the Author or the Author's employer or through digital repositories including, but not limited to, those maintained by CIC institutions, scholarly societies or funding agencies.

3. The Author further retains all non-exclusive rights necessary to grant to the Author's employing institution the non-exclusive right to use, reproduce, distribute, display, publicly perform, and make copies of the work in electronic, digital or in print form in connection with teaching, conference presentations, lectures, other scholarly works, and all academic and professional activities conducted at the Author's employing institution.

THIS ADDENDUM AND THE PUBLICATION AGREEMENT, TAKEN TOGETHER, CONSTITUTE THE FINAL AGREEMENT BETWEEN THE AUTHOR AND THE PUBLISHER WITH RESPECT TO THE PUBLICATION OF THE ARTICLE AND ALLOCATION OF RIGHTS UNDER COPYRIGHT IN THE ARTICLE. ANY MODIFICATION OF OR ADDITIONS TO THE TERMS OF THIS AMENDMENT OR TO THE PUBLICATION AGREEMENT MUST BE IN WRITING AND EXECUTED BY BOTH PUBLISHER AND AUTHOR IN ORDER TO BE EFFECTIVE.

AUTHOR                                    PUBLISHER

_____           _____
(Corresponding Author, on behalf of all authors)


_____           _____
Date                                      Date

[3] The 15 member universities of the Committee on Institutional Cooperation (CIC) are: University of Chicago; University of Illinois; Indiana University; University of Iowa; University of Maryland' University of Michigan; Michigan State University; University of Minnesota; University of Nebraska – Lincoln; Northwestern University; The Ohio State University; The Pennsylvania State University; Purdue University; Rutgers University; University of Wisconsin-Madison.

# Bibliography

Agence France Presse v. Daniel Morel v. Getty Images, et al., 934 F.Supp.2d 547 (S.D.N.Y. January 14, 2013).

Agreement on Guidelines for Classroom Copying in Not-For-Profit Educational Institutions with Respect to Books and Periodicals, March 1976 (U.S. Congress House. Copyright Law Revision, 94th Cong., 2d sess. [1976]. H. Doc. 1476; 68–70).

Albanese, A. R. "A Failure to Communicate." *Publishers Weekly*, June 14, 2010. Accessed April 10, 2014. http://www.publishersweekly.com/pw/by-topic/industry -news/publisher-news/article/43500-a-failure-to-communicate.html.

Albitz, Rebecca S. "Copyright Information Management and the University Library: Staffing, Organizational Placement and Authority." *The Journal of Academic Librarianship* 39 (2013): 429–35.

Allen, I. Elaine and Jeff Seaman. *Grade Change: Tracking Online Education in the United States*. Waltham, MA: Babson Survey Research Group. 2014. Accessed April 10, 2014. http://www.onlinelearningsurvey.com/reports/gradechange.pdf.

American Geophysical Union v. Texaco, Inc., 60 F.3d 913 (2d Cir. 1994), cert. dismissed, 516 U.S. 1005 (1995).

American Library Association. "Campus Copyright Librarian, John F. Reed Library, Fort Lewis College." *JobLIST*. Accessed January 13, 2014. http://joblist.ala.org/modules/jobseeker/Campus-Copyright-Librarian/24968.cfm.

American Library Association. "Manhattan College, Director, O'Malley Library." *JobLIST*. Accessed January 13, 2014. http://joblist.ala.org/modules/jobseeker/Director--OMalley-Library/24780.cfm.

American Library Association. "The Ohio State University Health Sciences Library." *JobLIST*. Accessed January 13, 2014. http://joblist.ala.org/modules/job seeker/Research-and-Education-Librarian-/24942.cfm.

American Library Association. "Texas A&M University-Corpus Christi, Director, Mary and Jeff Bell Library." *JobLIST*. Accessed January 13, 2014. http://joblist .ala.org/modules/jobseeker/Director-Mary-and-Jeff-Bell-Library/24755.cfm.

American Library Association. "University of Texas at Arlington Libraries, Director of Scholarly Communication." *JobLIST.* Accessed January 13, 2014. http://joblist .ala.org/modules/jobseeker/Director-of-Scholarly-Communication/24917.cfm.

American Library Association. "Western Washington University, Scholarly Communications Librarian." *JobLIST.* Accessed January 13, 2014. http://joblist.ala.org/ modules/jobseeker/Scholarly-Communications-Librarian/24759.cfm.

American Library Association. "State of America's Libraries Report 2013." *American Library Association.* Accessed April 8, 2014. http://www.ala.org/news/state -americas-libraries-report-2013/ebooks-and-copyright-issues.

Americans with Disabilities Act of 1990, Pub. L. 101-336, 104 Stat. 327 (1990), codified at 42 U.S.C. 12101 et seq.

Association for Information Media and Equipment v. Regents of the University of California, No. CV 10-9378 CBM (MANx) (C.D. Cal. Oct. 3, 2011). 2012 U.S. Dist. LEXIS 187811 (C.D. Cal. Nov. 20, 2012).

Association of College and Research Libraries Scholarly Communications Committee. "Principles and Strategies for the Reform of Scholarly Communication 1." *Association of College and Research Libraries,* 2003. http://www.ala.org/acrl/ publications/whitepapers/principlesstrategies.

Association of Public and Land-Grant Universities. "About Us." *Association of Public and Land-Grant Universities.* Accessed April 9, 2014. http://www.aplu.org/ page.aspx?pid=1565.

Association of Research Libraries. "Code of Best Practices in Fair Use for Academic and Research Libraries." *Association of Research Libraries,* January 2012. Accessed April 10, 2014. http://www.arl.org/storage/documents/publications/code -of-best-practices-fair-use.pdf.

Association of Research Libraries. "Colorado State University Morgan Library, Assistant Dean for Scholarly Communions and Collection Development." *Association of Research Libraries.* Accessed January 7, 2014. http://www.arl.org/ leadership-recruitment/job-listings/record/a0Id000000CHrkUEAT.

Aufderheide, Patricia, Peter Jaszi, Bryan Bello, and Tijana Milosevic. "Copyright, Permissions, and Fair Use among Visual Artists and the Academic and Museum Visual Arts Communities: An Issues Report." *College Art Association,* February 2014. Accessed April 10, 2014. http://www.collegeart.org/pdf/FairUseIssues Report.pdf.

Authors Guild, Inc. v. Google, 721 F. 3d 132 (2d Cir. 2013).

Authors Guild, Inc. v. HathiTrust, 902 F.Supp. 2d 445 (2012).

Basic Books, Inc. v. Kinko's Graphics Corporation, 758 F.Supp. 1522 (S.D.N.Y. 1991).

Beadon, Leigh. "Bob Goodlatte Calls for Copyright Reform, Leaves Specifics to the Imagination." *Techdirt,* April 24, 2013. Accessed April 10, 2014. http://www.tech-dirt.com/articles/20130424/13183222824/bob-goodlatte-calls-copyright-reform-leaves-specifics-to-imagination.shtml.

Beaubien, Anne K., Marlayna Christensen, Jennifer Kuehn, David K. Larsen, and May Lehane. "White Paper: International Interlibrary Loan." *Research Library Issues: A Quarterly Report from ARL, CNI, and SPARC,* no. 275 (June 2011): 7–14. Accessed April 10, 2014. http://publications.arl.org/rli275/.

BellSouth Advertising & Publishing Corporation v. Donnelly Information Publishing, Inc., 999 F.2d 1436 (11th Cir. 1993).

Berne Convention for the Protection of Literary & Artistic Works Implementation Act, Pub. L. 100-568, Stat. 102 (1988).

Bloom, Theo. "Data Access for the Open Access Literature: PLOS's Data Policy." *PLOS*, December 12, 2013. Accessed April 10, 2014. http://www.plos.org/data -access-for-the-open-access-literature-ploss-data-policy/.

Bouchoux, Deborah E. *Intellectual Property: The Law of Trademarks, Copyrights, Patents, and Trade Secrets*, 4th ed. Clifton Park, NY: Delmar Cengage Learning, 2013.

Bridgeman Art Library, Ltd. v. Corel Corporation, 36 F.Supp.2d 191 (1999).

Brigham Young University. "About Us." *BYU Copyright Licensing Office*. Accessed April 10, 2014. http://lib.byu.edu/sites/copyright/about/.

Brown, M. A. "Copyright Exceptions for Libraries in the Digital Age: U.S. Copyright Office Considers Reform of Section 108, Highlights of the Symposium." *College and Research Libraries News* 74, no. 4 (2013): 199–214. Accessed April 10, 2014. http://crln.acrl.org/content/74/4/199.full.

Burrow Giles Lithograph Company v. Sarony, 111 U.S. 53 (1884).

Butler, Brandon, Kenneth D. Crews, Donna Ferullo, and Kevin L. Smith. "White Paper: US Law and International Interlibrary Loan." *Research Library Issues: A Quarterly Report from ARL, CNI, and SPARC*, no. 275 (June 2011): 15–18. Accessed April 10, 2014. http://publications.arl.org/rli275/.

Buttler, Dwayne K. "Intimacy Gone Awry: Copyright and Special Collections." *Journal of Library Administration* 52 (2012): 279–93.

Buttler, Dwayne K. "Music and Copyright." In *Copyright Law for Librarians and Educators: Creative Strategies and Practical Solutions.* Edited by Kenneth D. Crews (Chicago: American Library Association, 2012).

Cambridge University Press et al v. Becker, 863 F.Supp.2d 1190 (N.D. Ga., May 11, 2012).

Campbell v. Acuff-Rose Music, Inc., 510 U.S. 569 (1994).

Capitol Records, LLC v. ReDigi Inc. 934 F.Supp.2d 640 (S.S.N.Y. 2013).

Cassedy, Claire. "Discussion on Orphan Works and Mass Digitization at U.S. Copyright Office, March 10–11, 2014." *Knowledge Economy International*, March 17, 2014. Accessed April 10, 2014. http://keionline.org/node/1978.

Center for Social Media. *Code of Best Practices in Fair Use for Media Literacy Education*. Washington DC: Center for Social Media, 2008. Accessed April 10, 2014. http://mediaeducationlab.com/sites/mediaeducationlab.com/files/CodeofBestPrac ticesinFairUse_0.pdf.

Center for Social Media. *Code of Best Practices in Fair Use for OpenCourseWare*. Washington DC: Center for Social Media, 2009. Accessed April 10, 2014. http:// www.cmsimpact.org/sites/default/files/10-305-OCW-Oct29.pdf.

Center for Social Media. *Code of Best Practices in Fair Use for Poetry.* Washington, DC: Center for Social Media, 2011. Accessed April 10, 2014. http://www.cmsim pact.org/sites/default/files/documents/pages/fairusepoetrybooklet_singlepg_3.pdf.

Chappell, Bill. 2013. "Record Number of International Students Attend U.S. Colleges." *NPR*, November 11. Accessed April 10, 2014. http://www.npr.org/blogs/

thetwo-way/2013/11/11/244601986/record-number-of-international-students
-attend-u-s-colleges.

Chronicle of Higher Education. "University of Notre Dame, Copyright and Licensing Librarian." Accessed February 11, 2014. https://chroniclevitae.com/jobs/0000819098-01.

Clement, Gail P. "American ETD Dissemination in the Age of Open Access." *C&RL News* 74 no. 11 (2013): 562–66.

Committee on Institutional Cooperation. "CIC Author's Addendum Brochure." Accessed April 9, 2014. http://www.cic.net/projects/library/scholarly-communication/authors-addendum-brochure.

Creative Commons. "Examples of Creative Commons License Use." Accessed April 9, 2014. http://creativecommons.org/examples.

Crespin, Margo E. *A Second Bite of the Apple: A Guide to Terminating Transfers under Section 203 of the Copyright Act.* New York: The Authors Guild, 2005. Accessed April 10, 2014. http://www.authorsguild.org/services/legal-services/terminating-transfers/.

Crews, Kenneth D. "The Copyright Management Center at IUPUI: Brief History, Dynamic Changes, and Future Demands." *Indiana Libraries: Journal of the Indiana Library Federation & the Indiana State Library* 19 (1 November 2000): 13–15.

Crews, Kenneth D. "Copyright, Fair Use, and Education." *Columbia University Copyright Advisory Office.* Accessed April 10, 2014. http://copyright.columbia.edu/copyright/.

Crews, Kenneth D. *Copyright Law for Librarians and Educators: Creative Strategies and Practical Solutions.* Chicago: American Library Association, 2012.

Dance Heritage Coalition. *Statement of Best Practices in Fair Use of Dance-Related Materials.* Washington, DC: Dance Heritage Coalition. http://www.cmsimpact.org/sites/default/files/documents/pages/DHC_fair_use_statement.pdf.

Dillinger, LLC v. Electronic Arts, Inc., 795 F.Supp.2d 829 (USDC S.D. Indiana, 2011).

Diversey v. Schmidly et al., 738 F.3d 1196 (10th Cir. 2013).

Duke University. "Office of Copyright and Scholarly Communications." *Duke University Libraries.* Accessed April 10, 2014. http://library.duke.edu/about/depts/scholcomm.

Economics and Statistics Administration and the United States Patent and Trademark Office. *Intellectual Property and the U.S. Economy: Industries in Focus.* Washington, DC: U. S. Department of Commerce, 2012. Accessed April 10, 2014. http://www.uspto.gov/news/publications/IP_Report_March_2012.pdf.

Educause. "7 Things You Should Know about the P2P Provisions of the HEOA." Accessed April 9, 2014. http://www.educause.edu/library/resources/7-things-you-should-know-about-p2p-provisions-heoa.

Educause. "Copyright Challenges in a MOOC Environment." Accessed April 9, 2014. http://www.educause.edu/library/resources/copyright-challenges-mooc-environment.

Educause. " Legal Sources of Online Content." Accessed April 10, 2014. http://www.educause.edu/focus-areas-and-initiatives/policy-and-security/educause-policy/issues-and-positions/intellectual-property/legal-sources-online.

Electronic Frontier Foundation. *RIAA v. The People: Five Years Later.* September 30, 2008. Accessed April 10, 2014. https://www.eff.org/wp/riaa-v-people-five -years-later.

Eldred v. Ashcroft, 537 U.S. 186 (2003).

Faden, Eric. "A Fair(y) Use Tale." *YouTube.* Accessed April 9, 2014. http://www .youtube.com/watch?v=CJn_jC4FNDo.

Fair Access to Science and Technology Research Act of 2013. H.R. 708, 113th Congress. 2013–2014.

Faulkner Literary Rights, LLC v. Sony Pictures Classics, Inc. 953 F.Supp.2d 701 (N.D. Miss. July 18, 2013).

Feist Publications, Inc. v. Rural Telephone Service Co., Inc. 499 U.S. 340 (1991).

Florida Department of State, Division of Library and Information Services, 2014. "Copyright Officer (Attorney)." *Nova Southeastern University.* Accessed April 10, 2014. http://www.floridalibraryjobs.org/index.cfm?fuseaction=job .view&jobID=4440&.

Folsom v. Marsh, 9 F.Cas. 342 (C.C.D. Mass. 1841).

Gardner, Eriq. "Sony Pictures Wins '*Midnight in Paris*' Lawsuit over Faulkner Quote (Exclusive)." *Hollywood Reporter*, July 18, 2013. Accessed April 10, 2014. http:// www.hollywoodreporter.com/thr-esq/sony-pictures-wins-midnight-paris-588515.

Gasaway, Laura N. *Copyright Questions and Answers for Information Professionals: From the Columns of Against the Grain.* West Lafayette, IN: Purdue University Press, 2013.

Gasaway, Lolly. "When U.S. Works Pass into the Public Domain." *University of North Carolina*, 2003. Accessed April 10, 2014. http://www.unc.edu/~unclng/ public-d.htm.

Georgetown University Intellectual Property. *Georgetown University Intellectual Property.* Washington DC: Georgetown University. http://studentaffairs .georgetown.edu/studentaffairs/policies/studentconduct/intellectualproperty/docu ment/1242777712827/Intellectual-Property-Policy.pdf.

Georgia State University Fair Use Check List. Accessed April 10, 2014. http://www .usg.edu/copyright/fair_use_checklist/. Adapted from Crews, K. and Buttler, D. Fair Use Checklist. Accessed April 10, 2014. http://copyright.columbia.edu/copy right/fair-use/fair-use-checklist/.

Google. "Company." Accessed April 9, 2014. http://www.google.com/about/ company/.

Hamilton College. *Policy on College-Owned Intellectual Property.* Clinton, NY: Hamilton College, 2005. Accessed April 10, 2014. https://my.hamilton.edu/ documents/IP_policy_collegeowned1.pdf.

Hamilton College. *Policy on the Determination of Ownership of Intellectual Property (IP).* Clinton, NY: Hamilton College, 2005. Accessed April 10, 2014. https:// my.hamilton.edu/documents/IP_policy_final_dec20051.pdf.

Harper, Georgia K. "Copyright Crash Course." *University of Texas at Austin.* Accessed April 10, 2014. http://copyright.lib.utexas.edu/.

Harper & Row Publishers, Inc. v. Nation Enterprises, 471 U.S. 539 (1985).

Harvard University. "About Us." *Harvard University Office of Technology Development.* Accessed April 9, 2014. http://otd.harvard.edu/about/.

Harvard University. "Office for Scholarly Communication." *Harvard University Library.* Accessed April 10, 2014. https://osc.hul.harvard.edu/osc-staff.

Hasan, Russell K. "Winning the Copyright War: Copyright's Merger Doctrine and Natural Rights Theory as Solutions to the Problem of Reconciling Copyright and Free Speech." *Engage* 14 no. 1 (2013). Accessed April 10, 2014. http://www.fed-soc.org/publications/detail/winning-the-copyright-war-copyrights-merger-doctrine-and-natural-rights-theory-as-solutions-to-the-problem-of-reconciling-copyright-and-free-speech.

HathiTrust Digital Library. "Mission Goals." Accessed April 9, 2014. http://www.hathitrust.org/mission_goals.

Higher Education Opportunity Act of 2008, Pub. L.110-315, 122 Stat. 3078 (2008), 20 *U.S.C.* § 1001 et seq.

Hirtle, Peter B. *Copyright Term and the Public Domain in the United States: 1 January 2014.* Ithaca: Cornell Copyright Information Center, 2014. Accessed April 10, 2014. http://copyright.cornell.edu/resources/publicdomain.cfm.

Ho v. Taflove, 648 F.3d 489 (7th Cir. 2011).

Hoon, Peggy. 2003. "The Original TEACH Act Toolkit." *J. Murrey Atkins Library, University of North Carolina at Charlotte.* Accessed April 10, 2014. http://copyright.uncc.edu/copyright/TEACH.

Huffington Post. April 29, 2013. "10 Universities That Receive the Most Government Money: 24/7 Wall Street." *Huffington Post* (blog). Accessed April 10, 2014. http://www.huffingtonpost.com/2013/04/27/universities-government-money_n_3165186.html.

Kelly v. Arriba Soft Corporation, 336 F.3d 811 (9th Cir. 2003).

Kirkpatrick, David D. "Historian's Fight for Her Reputation May Be Damaging It." *New York Times*, March 31, 2002. Accessed April 10, 2014. http://www.nytimes.com/2002/03/31/us/historian-s-fight-for-her-reputation-may-be-damaging-it.html.

Kirtsaeng v. John Wiley & Sons, Inc. 133 S.Ct. 1351 (2013).

Kolowich, Steve. "Doubts about MOOC's Continue to Rise, Survey Finds." *Chronicle of Higher Education*, January 15, 2014. Accessed April 10, 2014. https://chronicle.com/article/Doubts-About-MOOCs-Continue-to/144007/.

Kosur, James. "Daniel Morel's Twitter Photos Sold without Permission, $1.2 Million Awarded." *Social News Daily*, November 22, 2013. Accessed April 9, 2014. http://socialnewsdaily.com/19909/daniel-morels-twitter-photos-sold-without-permission-1-2-million-awarded/.

The Lanham Act, Pub. L. 79-489, 60 Stat. 427 (1946), 15 U.S.C. § 1051 et seq.

Leahy-Smith America Invents Act, Pub. L. 112-29, 125 Stat. 284 (2011).

Lewis, Mark. "Ambrose Problems Date Back to Ph.D. Thesis." *Forbes*, May 10, 2002. Accessed April 10, 2014. http://www.forbes.com/2002/05/10/0510ambrose.html.

Library Copyright Alliance. "Before the House Committee on the Judiciary Subcommittee on Courts, Intellectual Property and the Internet; Hearing on the Scope of Fair Use." January 28, 2014. http://www.librarycopyrightalliance.org/bm~doc/stfairusepsarev.pdf.

Lipinski, Tomas A. *The Librarian's Legal Companion for Licensing Information Resources and Services*. Chicago: ALA-Neal-Schuman, 2013. http://www.alastore.ala.org/pdf/9781555706104_excerpt.pdf.

Massachusetts Institute of Technology. "Ownership of Intellectual Property." *MIT Policies and Procedures*. Accessed April 10, 2014. http://web.mit.edu/policies/13/13.1.html.

McCord, Gretchen. "What Is a Copyright Officer?" *Gretchen McCord: Copyright Officer on Call*. Accessed April 9. 2014. http://www.copyrightofficeroncall.com.

Morrill Act, Pub. L. 37-108 (1862); 7 U.S.C. § 301 et seq.

Mullin, Joe. "Heirs of Superman Artist Can't Reclaim Their Copyright, Judge Rules." *Arts Technica*, October 18, 2012. Accessed April 10, 2014. http://arstechnica.com/tech-policy/2012/10/heirs-of-superman-artist-cant-reclaim-their-copyright-judge-rules/.

Mullins, J. L., C. Murray-Rust, J. L. Ogburn, R. Crow, O. Ivins, A. Mower, D. Nesdill, M. P. Newton, J. Speer, and C. Watkinson. *Library Publishing Services: Strategies for Success: Final Research Report*. Washington, DC: SPARC, 2012.

National Center for Education Statistics. "Table 220: Historical Summary of Faculty, Enrollment, Degrees, and Finances in Degree Granting Institutions: Selected Years, 1869–70 through 2010–11." In *Digest of Education Statistics*. Washington, DC: United States Department of Education, 2013. Accessed April 10, 2014. http://nces.ed.gov/programs/digest/d12/tables/dt12_220.asp.

New York Post. "Marvel to Keep Spider-Man, X-Men Rights after Family of Original Artist Sues to Terminate Comic Giant's Copyrights—Agree Work Was 'for Hire.'" *New York Post*, August 8, 2013. Accessed April 10, 2014. http://nypost.com/2013/08/08/marvel-to-keep-spider-man-x-men-rights-after-family-of-original-artist-sues-to-terminate-comic-giants-copyrights-agree-work-was-for-hire/.

North American Free Trade Agreement Act, Pub. L. 103-182, Stat. 107 (1993).

Notices of Termination of Transfer and Licenses. 37 Code of Federal Regulations §201.10.

Pallante, M. A. "The Next Great Copyright Act." *Columbia Journal of Law and the Arts* 36 no.3 (2013): 315–44. Accessed April 10, 2014. http://www.copyright.gov/docs/next_great_copyright_act.pdf.

Panzar, J. "Large Finc Upheld against BU Grad for Illegal Song Downloads." *Boston Globe*, June 27, 2013. Accessed August 26, 2013. http://www.bostonglobe.com/metro/2013/06/26/court-upholds-fine-against-former-student-for-illegal-music-downloads/aXul4dPHxzv5mrnDUehaEN/story.html.

Park, Kevin. "From Ray Charles to 'Y.M.C.A.'—Section 203 Copyright Terminations in 2013 and Beyond." *The IP Litigator: Devoted to Intellectual Property Litigation and Enforcement* 19 no. 2 (Mar/Apr 2013): 7–12.

Pennsylvania State University. "Copyright Officer, University Park." *Pennsylvania State University Libraries*. Accessed April 10, 2014. https://www.libraries.psu.edu/psul/jobs/facjobs/copy.html.

Peterson, Andrea. "How One Publisher Is Stopping Academics from Sharing Their Research." *Washington Post*, December 19, 2013. Accessed April 10, 2014. http://

www.washingtonpost.com/blogs/the-switch/wp/2013/12/19/how-one-publisher-is -stopping-academics-from-sharing-their-research/.

Princeton University Press v. Michigan Document Services, Inc., 99 F.3d 1381 (6th Cir. 1996), *cert. denied*, 520 U.S. 1156 (1997).

Purdue University. "Purdue University Policies: Intellectual Property (I.A.I.)." Accessed April 10, 2014. http://www.purdue.edu/policies/academic-research-affairs/ ia1.html.

Purdue University Libraries. "Director, University Copyright Office." *Chronicle of Higher Education*. Accessed September 9, 1999. http://chronicle.com/free/jobs/ admin/legal/12145.html.

Rainie, Lee, and Maeve Duggan. *E-Book Reading Jumps; Print Book Reading Declines*. Washington, DC: Pew Internet and American Life Project, 2012. Accessed April 10, 2014. http://libraries.pewinternet.org/2012/12/27/e-book-reading-jumps -print-book-reading-declines/.

Rice, L. "C.U. Changes E-Reserve Policy to Avoid Lawsuit." *Cornell Daily Sun*, October 3, 2006. Accessed April 10, 2014. http://cornellsun.com/node/18733.

Rights of Publicity. Indiana Code § 32-36-1-8(a).

Rohter, Larry. "A Copyright Victory 35 Years Later." *New York Times*, September 10, 2013. Accessed April 10, 2014. http://www.nytimes.com/2013/09/11/arts/ music/a-copyright-victory-35-years-later.html?_r=0.

Salinger v. Random House, Inc. 811 F.2d 90 (2d Cir. 1987).

Schwartz, Meredith. "ARL Launches Library-Led Solution to Federal Open Access Requirements." *Library Journal*, June 12, 2013. Accessed April 10, 2014. http://lj.libraryjournal.com/2013/06/oa/arl-launches-library-led-solution-to-federal -open-access-requirements/.

Schwartz, Meredith, and Gary Price. "Judge's Ruling a Win for Fair Use in Authors Guild v. HathiTrust Case." *Library Journal Infodocket*, October 10, 2012. Accessed April 10, 2014. http://www.infodocket.com/2012/10/10/judge-rules-on -authors-guild-v-hathitrust/.

Shieber, Stuart M. *A Model Open-Access Policy, version 1.1*. Cambridge, MA: Harvard University, 2013. Accessed April 10, 2014. https://osc.hul.harvard.edu/sites/ default/files/model-policy-annotated_01_2013.pdf.

Sonny Bono Copyright Term Extension Act, Pub. L. 105-298, Stat. 112 (1998).

SPARC. "Author's Rights: The SPARC Author Addendum." *SPARC*. Accessed April 10, 2014. http://www.sparc.arl.org/initiatives/author-rights.

Stanford University. "Copyright Renewal Database." *Libraries & Academic Information Resources*. Accessed April 10, 2014. http://collections.stanford.edu/copyright -renewals/bin/page?forward=home.

Statute of Anne, 8 Anne, c. 19 (1710). Accessed April 10, 2014. http://avalon.law .yale.edu/18th_century/anne_1710.asp.

Stebbins, Michael. "Expanding Public Access to the results of Federally Funded Research." *U.S. Office of Science and Technology Policy* (blog), February 22, 2013. Accessed April 10, 2014. http://www.whitehouse.gov/blog/2013/02/22/expanding -public-access-results-federally-funded-research.

Technology, Education and Copyright Harmonization Act, Pub. L. 107-273, Stat. 116 (2002), codified at 17 U.S.C. §§ 110(2) and 112(f).

United States Copyright Office. *Report on Orphan Works: A Report of the Register of Copyrights.* Washington DC: Library of Congress, 2006. Accessed April 10, 2014. http://www.copyright.gov/orphan/orphan-report.pdf.

United States Copyright Office. *Legal Issues in Mass Digitization: A Preliminary Analysis and Discussion Document.* Washington DC: United States Copyright Office, 2011. Accessed April 10, 2014. http://www.copyright.gov/docs/massdigitization/USCOMassDigitization_October2011.pdf.

United States Copyright Office. "Notice of Inquiry, Orphan Works and Mass Digitization." *Federal Register* 77, no. 204 (October 22, 2012). Accessed April 10, 2014. http://www.copyright.gov/fedreg/2012/77fr64555.pdf.

University of California, Los Angeles. "About Us." *University of California, Los Angeles Office of Intellectual Property & Industry Sponsored Research.* Accessed April 10, 2014. http://oip.ucla.edu/about-us.

University of Notre Dame. "Office of Technology Transfer." Accessed April 10, 2014. http://ott.nd.edu/.

University of Ottawa. "Copyright Officer, Manager of Copyright Services." *Careers and Jobs.* Accessed April 10, 2014. https://client.njoyn.com/CL2/xweb/Xweb.asp?tbtoken=YF9bRhoXCGgHZ3ACMCZUCCA7AWREcCJUB0ggUFoME2VfLzU TK0YSBhNxcAkbVhJSQXEqWA%3D%3D&chk=dFlbQBJe&clid=27081&Page =jobdetails&jobid=J0113-0072.

University System of Georgia. "Fair Use Check List." *USG Copyright Policy.* Accessed April 10, 2014. http://www.usg.edu/copyright/fair_use_checklist/.

University System of Georgia. "Policy on the Use of Copyrighted Works in Education and Research." *USG Copyright Policy.* Accessed April 10, 2014. http://www.usg.edu/copyright/.

Uruguay Round Agreements Act, Pub. L. 103-465, Stat. 108 (1994).

U.S. Const. art. 1, §. 8, cl. 8.

U.S. Copyright Act, 17 U.S.C. § 101.

U.S. Copyright Act, 17 U.S.C. § 101 et seq.

U.S. Copyright Act, 17 U.S.C. § 102(a).

U.S. Copyright Act, 17 U.S.C. § 102(b).

U.S. Copyright Act, 17 U.S.C. § 106.

U.S. Copyright Act, 17 U.S.C. § 107.

U.S. Copyright Act, 17 U.S.C. § 108.

U.S. Copyright Act, 17 U.S.C. § 108(a) (3).

U.S. Copyright Act, 17 U.S.C. § 108(b)(2).

U.S. Copyright Act, 17 U.S.C. § 108(d).

U.S. Copyright Act, 17 U.S.C. § 108(i).

U.S. Copyright Act, 17 U.S.C. § 110(2)(D)(i).

U.S. Copyright Act, 17 U.S.C. § 121.

U.S. Copyright Act, 17 U.S.C. § 504.

U.S. Copyright Act, 17 U.S.C. § 1201.

U.S. National Commission on New Technological Uses of Copyrighted Works. *Final Report*. Washington, DC: Library of Congress, 1979.

Washington and Lee University. "Policy for the Use of Copyrighted Works." *Code of Policies.* Accessed April 10, 2014. http://www2.wlu.edu/x30754.xml.

World Intellectual Property Organization. "Marrakesh Treaty to Facilitate Access to Published Works for Persons Who Are Blind, Visually Impaired, or Otherwise Print Disabled." *World Intellectual Property Organization*. Accessed April 10, 2014. http://www.wipo.int/meetings/en/doc_details.jsp?doc_id=245323.

Yale University, Division of the Vice President and General Counsel. "Copyright: Academic Copying and Student Course Packets." Accessed April 10, 2014. http://ogc.yale.edu/copyright-academic-copying-and-student-course-packets.

# Index

# About the Author

Donna L. Ferullo is the director of the University Copyright Office at Purdue University and is also associate professor of library science. Ms. Ferullo advises the university on copyright compliance issues and is responsible for educating the Purdue University community on their rights and responsibilities under the copyright law.

Ms. Ferullo holds a doctor of jurisprudence degree from Suffolk University Law School in Boston, Massachusetts, and a masters of library science degree from the University of Maryland in College Park, Maryland. She is a member of the Massachusetts Bar and the United States Supreme Court Bar.

CPSIA information can be obtained at www.ICGtesting.com
Printed in the USA
LVOW11*0300301014

411152LV00010B/87/P